BUILDING LASTING BRIDGES

An Updated Handbook for
Intercultural Ministries

Kathryn Choy-Wong
Lucia Ann McSpadden
Dale M. Weatherspoon

Building Lasting Bridges: An Updated Handbook for Intercultural Ministries

Interior design by Beth Oberholtzer.
Cover design by Danny Ellison.

Library of Congress Cataloging-in-Publication data

Names: Choy-Wong, Kathryn, author. | McSpadden, Lucia Ann, author. | Weatherspoon, Dale M., author.

Title: Building lasting bridges : an updated handbook for intercultural ministries / Kathryn Choy-Wong, Lucia Ann McSpadden, Dale M Weatherspoon.

Other titles: Building bridges

Description: Valley Forge, PA : Judson Press, [2022]

Identifiers: LCCN 2022014644 (print) | LCCN 2022014645 (ebook) | ISBN 9780817018368 (paperback) | ISBN 9780817082451 (epub)

Subjects: LCSH: Church work with minorities--Christianity. | Race relations--Religious aspects--Christianity. | Ethnic relations--Religious aspects--Christianity.

Classification: LCC BV4468 .C56 2022 (print) | LCC BV4468 (ebook) | DDC 259.089--dc23/eng/20220622

LC record available at https://lccn.loc.gov/2022014644

LC ebook record available at https://lccn.loc.gov/2022014645

Printed in the U.S.A.

First printing, 2022.

Contents

Note

To benefit fully from this book it is recommended that you access the workbook titled *Building Lasting Bridges Workbook* online. It will be helpful to review the exercises and other materials that accompany each chapter, as well as the appendices. The workbook may be viewed at www.judsonpress.com. All supplemental materials and exercises are identified online by the book chapter to which they correspond. Exercises and additional resources are noted by their corresponding book chapter and titles.

In addition to having a device to access the online material, you may want to keep a digital or hard copy of the Bible alongside *Building Lasting Bridges* because reading the selected texts will give you a greater appreciation and understanding of the discussions that follow.

Acknowledgments

I give special thanks to Taylor Jung for her tireless efforts in research and assistance in obtaining copyright permission.

Thank you to my family for taking over family chores while I was writing, and to my husband, Arthur, and my son, Jordan. —Katie

Thank you to my family for providing the life framework for my journey. —Shan

Thank you to my family for walking this journey alongside me. —Dale

Thank you to our colleagues in the former i-Relate Institute for the twenty-plus years in intercultural training.

Thank you to two denominations for their intercultural work: American Baptist Churches USA and its American Baptist Home Mission Societies; The United Methodist Church and its California-Nevada Annual Conference, Conference Commission on Religion and Race; and The General Board of Higher Education and Ministry.

Thank you to Rev. Arthur Gafke, former executive with the General Board of Higher Education and Ministry, who envisioned, enabled, and guided the cross-cultural/cross-racial research that provided rich insights for our work.

Thank you to the churches in California with whom we ministered interculturally: New Life Christian Fellowship in Castro Valley, Almaden Hills UMC, Redwood City First UMC, Alum Rock UMC, Good Samaritan UMC, and Easter Hill UMC.

Introduction

This book is a guide for individuals who desire to relate to one another interculturally, that is, learning to be sensitive and desiring to engage meaningfully across different cultures. It is designed to be a beginning point for those interested in intercultural work since much intercultural work is an accumulation of learning experiences.

This book is for you if:

you are interested in getting to know others of a different ethnic or cultural background than your own

you want to build bridges and form authentic relationships with persons of different ethnic or cultural heritages

you want to work with and alongside a diverse, ethnic, or cultural group of people

you are willing to live out the biblical mandate of "love your neighbor as yourself"

you are open to training and new ideas on living out God's vision of a community of reconciliation and love with all of God's people

you want to be a part of building a Beloved Community

This book is for you if you have any "buts":

I don't know anyone from another ethnic, racial, or cultural group than mine

I don't know how to begin

I am alone in my desire, and I don't have support from my own ethnic or cultural group

I don't have the time, this seems too demanding

I'm afraid

I don't want to make mistakes

I don't want to hurt or offend anyone

I don't know what to say or do

I don't understand others who are so different from me

I don't know who my neighbor is

The Making of Three Bridge People

Bridge persons are individuals who know their own culture so well that they understand why you could be confused by it. With that understanding, bridge persons are willing to help you learn about their culture's behavior and values, cultural expectations, and the "way things are done." Because bridge persons trust your concern, they are willing to take the time to guide and mentor you. Bridge persons truly are gifts in the journey to understanding.

Why should we desire to relate to other cultural or ethnic groups? Here are our personal stories.

Rev. Kathryn (Katie) Choy-Wong

I grew up with two brothers and a sister, of whom I am the oldest. My father came to the United States as an immigrant at the age of fourteen, alone. He came to join my grandfather, who was part owner of a Chinese American restaurant in Miles City, Montana. My mother was born in San Francisco at Chinese Hospital,[1] the same hospital where I would be born twenty-four years later. At the time of my mother's birth, this hospital was the only hospital for the Chinese because San Francisco was a segregated city. My mother remembers being confined to Chinatown, seeing beaches with signs of "No Chinese Allowed," and being threatened with a beating if she ventured outside of Chinatown into other neighborhoods.

Even though "officially" San Francisco was no longer segregated when I was born, I still felt like an outsider. I grew up in a predominantly black neighborhood where the elementary school was about 90 percent black. My best friend, who was African American,[2] lived across the street from me, so we played together practically every day.

I remember how happy we were when our parents bought each of us a Barbie doll. Here were two minorities, one African American and one Chinese American, playing with blonde Barbie dolls. Dolls that looked like us didn't exist. We didn't have money for doll clothes, so we would make clothes out of toilet paper, tissue, and paper napkins. We relied heavily on our imaginations, pretending what the dolls wore, and that the dolls looked like us.

When I was ten, my parents decided to move after it became dangerous in our neighborhood. Our flat was burglarized three times, and the owner of our neighborhood liquor store was shot and killed. Every weekend, we would look for houses in a suburb called South San Francisco (near the San Francisco airport), visiting the ones that displayed "For Sale" signs. My parents had saved enough money for a down payment, but each real estate agent or homeowner would tell us that we were too late; the house had just sold, yet the next weekend we would see the same houses with the same "For Sale" signs. We weren't aware of redlining at the time.[3] My parents finally found a house and an owner willing to sell at an affordable price: $17,000! That was still a large sum in 1963. My parents took out a thirty-year loan.

In my new neighborhood I went to a predominantly white American high school where I remember feeling like an outsider, especially when it came to dating. I didn't like myself because I didn't fit the ideal beauty portrayed in the media. I had black hair, a flat nose and chest, no double eyelids, and I was short. I didn't want to be different from my peers. I was ashamed of being Chinese. (Later I learned that this is called "internalized racism.")

However, I attended a Chinese American church in San Francisco, where I felt at home and didn't have to explain myself. I didn't have to feel odd using chopsticks, eating rice for dinner every night instead of potatoes or mac and cheese, celebrating Chinese festivals, or wearing a black armband for a month when my grandmother died.

It wasn't until I went to college that I finally accepted and affirmed who I was. I started college in 1971, several years after the Civil Rights Bill of 1964, and soon after the student protests at San Francisco State in 1969. As a result, I was able to take ethnic studies, and for the first time I began to learn about my own Asian American history and to understand systemic racism and its devastating impact.[4] I began to read about and hear from other students of color, and as I learned more, I appreciated the other cultures that surrounded me, and my being Asian American.

For the last twenty-plus years, my coauthors and I have been consulting and training in intercultural ministry with an institute we started, called i-Relate.[5] We have trained local pastors, laity, and denominational leaders in the United Methodist, American Baptist, and United Church of Christ denominations. It is this work that we bring to you in this book.

My life's journey has led me to believe in diversity, and that we are all better as a human race when we learn to understand and appreciate each other, advocate for those who have no voice, and confront stereotyping, prejudice, racism, injustice in our US culture, and in our political, societal, and religious institutions.

My hope is that your personal journey will also take you to a better place and empower you to make this world truly the "kingdom of heaven on earth" and the Beloved Community.

Rev. Dr. Dale M. Weatherspoon

I grew up in San Francisco in the 1960s as a young black man in a largely African American neighborhood. My immediate neighbors included German, French, Scottish, Maltese, and Italian families. Filipinos, Chinese, Japanese, and Hispanic families lived down the street and around the corner. Some families included mentally challenged persons. Most of the families were in the same economic bracket. All of the families that I can remember were two-parent working families. A few mothers were stay-at-home moms. There were no apartments. All of the homes were two- or three-bedroom houses. We didn't call it a multicultural neighborhood at the time. It was just a neighborhood, a culturally mixed neighborhood where most children played with each other and visited one another's homes. In my early adult years, I recognized that my first neighborhood had been a slice of heaven. That's how I first encountered the world. I wasn't aware that the rest of the world didn't experience the same thing.

We didn't use the word *multicultural* or *intercultural* back in the 1960s and 1970s. We used the word *mixed* to describe our neighborhood. During that time San Francisco was unique in that it had everybody from everywhere around the world. The church I attended was predominantly black but welcomed all people. We always had a few white Americans, as well as Asian, gay, and lesbian members. The world is even more pluralistic now than it was when I was growing up. Encountering people of other ethnicities is unavoidable unless you are consciously trying to avoid "the other."

As an elementary-age child, I would attend major league baseball games with my dad, who was a police officer and the second black police officer in the city's police department. When we attended the games, we sat with other police officers from the department. We were always the only blacks. Several blocks from my home there was a neighborhood called Hunter's Point. It was predominantly made up of blacks with a few "poor white folks." On Saturdays, I rode the bus to my music lessons in another part of San Francisco. Mostly blacks and some whites and Chinese boarded the bus where I boarded. People sat wherever they wanted, but most blacks sat in the back. Once the bus reached downtown, all the blacks disembarked except me. It was there that more Chinese and other whites boarded the bus heading toward two neighborhoods north of downtown: Chinatown and North Beach, where mostly the Chinese and Italians lived. This was my first awareness of segregated neighborhoods.

Years later, I recognized that I had my first encounter with racism when I was in the sixth grade and the captain of my elementary school's traffic squad. Each year all of the elementary and junior high school traffic squads would gather in Golden Gate Park for a major parade in front of the city's police chief and other dignitaries. I was excited that as the first captain I would be leading our school's traffic squad. Before that big day arrived one of my elementary school officials approached me. I don't recall if this person told me or asked me about the change that would take place, namely, that one of the other captains, a part Anglo, part Hispanic girl, had been made the first captain for the parade. The rationale was that boys could be on the traffic squad in junior high school, but not girls. This meant this was her only opportunity; I would have other chances in junior high school to lead the school's safety patrol in a parade.

I don't remember how I responded at that moment. I know that years later I still felt the hurt, anger, and disappointment. What made the official think I wanted to be on the traffic squad in junior high school, or that I would be first captain again even if I were on the traffic squad? My parents had taught me to be nice and compassionate, so at the time I behaved in an understanding and gracious manner. After all, the girl was my friend. In retrospect, I believe what happened wasn't fair. Someone may have thought the change was nice, but I felt as though my feelings were not taken into account. Whether intentional or unintentional, I believe I encountered a racist system and reverse sexism and was excluded from an honored leadership role and a memorable experience.

Now, I serve as a pastor in The United Methodist Church, a denomination that is predominately white but with many cultures from around the world as part of its membership. Effective communication seems to be the challenge. As one white American clergyperson put it, "Our denomination operates out of a European American perspective. The European Americans don't understand the cultural nuances." He added, "Unconsciously, the models of ministry used seek to assimilate the others." It often seems that the dominant culture doesn't think outside of the box very easily. Many white Americans as well as ethnic people in leadership who have been fully acculturated look at situations through the lenses of the dominant culture, white, European American lenses. Learning to ask new questions and look at situations through multiple lenses, lenses of other cultures and ethnicities, is crucial in this day and age.

Currently, I serve as pastor of an African American congregation in a multiethnic, multiracial community of the East Bay. I also serve in the California-Nevada Annual Conference, which contains approximately 360 churches composed of roughly twenty ethnic groups and numerous languages. There are about fifty-five pastors appointed and serving in congregations different from their ethnic or cultural backgrounds. Many more pastors will serve in such appointments. How does one prepare for such appointments? Some might say "carefully and prayerfully."

Because I see more and more pastors, leaders, and congregations desiring to be multiracial and intercultural, I want to share some of my experiences and those of others. My hope is that this book will offer some insights and help the reader ask different questions that lead to a fruitful ministry in the multiracial, intercultural context. I hope this book will also help members of congregations better understand the challenges, struggles, hopes, and dreams of doing intercultural ministry.

Dr. Lucia (Shan) Ann McSpadden

My growing up was very typical of a white, Euro-American, middle-class family in a suburban town in the 1950s. As my father advanced in his work with a publishing company, our family (my mother and father, my younger sister and I) moved almost every year—mostly living in small towns surrounding Detroit, Michigan, and a few times in New Jersey and Maryland. These were communities of single-family homes with lots of kids my own age to play with, and schools I could walk to from first grade onward without any parental supervision. I never saw nor was I aware of any "persons of color" or any non-Christian families. I attended Sunday school at times and, as I became an adolescent, various Methodist youth groups and summer camps. Mine was an insulated, homogeneous environment of white middle-class families who never noticed any social tensions or contradictions. I had a secure and socially unaware childhood as likely did most of my playmates.

However, there was an undercurrent of xenophobia in my family about which I gradually became aware. Anti-Catholic comments issued forth from both my parents. My mother was born and grew up on a single-family farm in New Brunswick, Canada, a province divided religiously and educationally between Protestant English-speaking and Roman Catholic French-speaking citizens. The "us-them" feelings were strong in both communities; for example, my grandfather told my mother that he would hit her if he ever saw her talking with a Catholic (even though he had never laid a hand on her)! I presume French-speaking parents were saying something similar to their children. Hearing these comments confused me, especially since I had never met nor did I know anything about Catholics. However, I learned early on that questioning my parents' actions, beliefs, or decisions was not acceptable.

My father was born in Liverpool, England, the son of a wealthy Englishman and an American mother. When he was twelve years old, his father died suddenly, and his mother took the five children and moved back to the United States. The family went abruptly from wealthy to penniless. The children were farmed out to relatives while my grandmother searched for employment. Gradually, the family was brought back together with a single mother supporting five children. Perhaps one might say they were working poor. My father, although working during college, had to drop out due to a lack of funds. With a sigh of sadness, my father mentioned this. My parents married in 1929, at the start of the Great Depression, which had a great impact on my father. My mother worked as a nurse while he was unemployed; he then worked going door to door to collect the weekly payment for magazine subscriptions. A thankless job, I imagine.

I mentioned my father's background because I believe it had a lifetime effect on his attitudes toward persons who were marginalized by race or religion in our society. Since he had worked up from nothing to a middle-class life—a Horatio Alger-type story—he believed that "anyone can do that if they are willing to work hard."

I was totally unaware of the racial dynamics in the US, in general, and especially in Detroit in the 1940s and 1950s. Although there was a brief two-day racial protest in downtown Detroit when I was in junior high, I was not aware of it.

Race was never a topic of conversation in our home. On occasions I would go with my dad to help in his office on a Saturday. Once I noticed a black man—"Negro" was the term at that time—come in response to a job ad in the *Detroit News*. My father and I were the only people in the office. My father responded to the man that the position had already been filled. I didn't think anything about that until later when a white man came in responding to the same ad. My father greeted him and gave him the forms to fill out. I was shocked since my parents were very clear that I was never to lie. Although nothing was said about race, my eleven-year-old mind understood clearly what had just happened.

Now I was really confused and very uneasy about these and other "anti-the-other" assertions from my parents. I have often reflected and wondered what guided me to reject these attitudes over time.

The answers are undoubtedly complex; however, a major influence was my Methodist youth group, its pastor (young and handsome), and the various related activities and opportunities. Several experiences in that context especially stand out in my memory as opening the world to me, deepening my faith, and raising questions. At one evening worship service that the youth were required to attend (and where we sat in the back and talked and passed notes), the preacher was a German Lutheran pastor from Hamburg, Germany. He spoke about the experience during the fire-bombing by the Allies late in World War II, describing in personal detail how over seventy-two hours he and his people lay in the basement of the church; when the bombing stopped, the city was enveloped in flames.[6] My gut response was, "Oh my gosh, Germans are people!"[7] The second experience was at a summer Methodist youth camp where I attended a class led by a Jewish rabbi. This deepened my faith as it was my first contact with a Jewish person, Jesus' people; my positive reaction strongly contrasted with my father's reactions and negative comments about Jews. Overall, summer camp was where I committed my life to Jesus and began to think seriously about what that might mean.

In my all-white high school and later in my all-white college I was fascinated with learning foreign languages (Latin and Spanish). My appetite for experiencing "the other" was sparked; I began seeking opportunities to meet and speak with Spanish speakers. In my context of Southern California, that meant Mexican and Mexican American persons. One summer I took inorganic chemistry at a college near my home. One of my classmates was a Mexican student with whom I worked closely in our chemistry lab. This led to studying together at my home, and our friendship grew. After a few weeks, my parents informed me that he was not welcome in our home because he was a

Mexican. I was horrified and deeply embarrassed; it was like a gut punch and fueled a strong awakening about racial injustice. This was the first time I was personally affected by my parents' hostility to "the other" and most especially toward "persons of color," although I didn't know that term at the time.

I believe that God shaped my journey. The gospel of Jesus has been my spiritual guide through the years. I am so grateful to those who have guided me, who have challenged me, who have educated me, and who have patiently and lovingly walked with me on this journey. I never imagined I would be so blessed as to be surrounded by such a diverse, loving, witnessing group of friends and colleagues. These mentors, people who will say, *Stop! Listen! Believe! Learn! Change! Act!* have been and continue to be my spiritual guides. Thanks be to God!

We, the authors, hope that this book will open doors for you to continue to grow in your understanding of yourself as an ethnic or cultural being as well as give you a deeper appreciation, sensitivity, and respect for others. This book is a tool, but with God's guidance and your own commitment, you can truly build bridges among God's human diversity toward a Beloved Community.

NOTES

1. The Tung Wah Dispensary, the predecessor to Chinese Hospital, was established in 1899 to provide healthcare services to the Chinese who faced discrimination and limited access to public services.

2. For our definition of black and African American, see the glossary at the end of the book.

3. Redlining is the systematic denial of sales and loans to people of color to keep certain areas of cities and towns white. The Civil Rights Act of 1964 and the Fair Housing Act of 1968 prohibit housing discrimination based on race, color, religion, sex, disability, familial status, or national origin.

4. If it weren't for an outstanding high school history teacher, I would never have heard about the 120,000 Japanese Americans

interned in the United States during World War II. Our US history books never mentioned the history of people of color or their contributions.

5. i-Relate.org was an institute primarily funded by the United Methodists for consulting, training, and resourcing local churches, pastors, and denominational leaders. The institute no longer exists.

6. As part of a sustained campaign of strategic bombing during World War II, the attack during the last week of July 1943, code-named Operation Gomorrah, created one of the largest firestorms raised by the Royal Air Force and United States Army Air Forces in World War II, killing an estimated 35,000 civilians and wounding 125,000 more in Hamburg, and virtually destroying most of the city (Wikipedia referencing Noble Frankland and Charles Webster, *The Strategic Air Offensive Against Germany, 1939–1945*, vol. 2: *Endeavour, Part 4* [London: Her Majesty's Stationery Office, 1961], 260–61).

7. In my family Germans were always referred to in a World War II context—the enemy, the Nazis, not as human beings.

PART 1

GOD'S STORY

Rev. Kathryn Choy-Wong

CHAPTER 1

Diversity in Our World

Have you ever wondered how diverse our world is, and why God made our world so diverse?

Walk into any large supermarket. Let's try the cereal aisle. Did you ever notice the different brands of cereal? Take Cheerios, for example. You might think that would keep your choices simple. However, to your dismay, you encounter not one or two or three types of Cheerios; instead you encounter many more. Alphabetically you encounter Apple Cinnamon, Banana Nut, Berry Burst (and this comes in Strawberry or Triple Berry), Blueberry, Cinnamon (and Cinnamon Burst), Cinnamon Nut, Cinnamon Oat Crunch, Chocolate, Chocolate Peanut Butter, Frosted, Fruity, Honey Nut, Honey Nut Medley Crunch, Maple, Multi-Grain, Multi-Grain Dark Chocolate Crunch, Multi-Grain Peanut Butter Crunch, Pumpkin Spice, Oat Cluster, Toasted Coconut, Very Berry, Yogurt Burst Strawberry, and Yogurt Burst Vanilla. Now you realize what you thought was going to be a simple purchase is monumental!

We should not be surprised. We humans can make anything complicated. But is that how God intended things to be?

When we look at our world and realize that God made it very complex we can be amazed at how diverse it really is. Each little creature, from microbes to the largest in the world, is so integrally entwined, so interconnected, so interdependent that when one is missing, all the others are affected.

And so it is with human beings as well. See Genesis 1:26-27, which tells us that in God's creation plan, we are part of God's diversity. God planned it that way. God created a diverse world of wonderful creatures and living things, including human beings. Each part of God's creation is related and important to the total creation. Everything is connected.

On the other hand, as human beings, we have a special connectedness to God, the Creator. Humankind is made in God's image. That means we reflect God. We have the ability to relate to God. We have the responsibility to respond to God. In that way, each one of us is the same. Humankind. We all have the potential to be fully loving and faithful to God. In God's eyes there are no differences that separate us from one another.

We all were born. As children, we all relied on receiving caring love from adults. As we mature, we all seek ways to learn and grow. We all want to be valued and respected. We all have hopes and dreams. We also are alike in that we are imperfect. We all make mistakes, fail, and learn from our errors. We begin to understand the meaning of God's forgiveness as we repent of our wrongdoing and receive God's grace in our lives. We are the same in our humanity.

Yet, just as God created diversity in the world, God created us with unique gifts and abilities that can be used to glorify God. Not one of us is exactly the same as anyone else in the world. Our physical makeup, our personalities, our natural talents, our limitations and weaknesses, our family upbringing, our social relationships, our opportunities and experiences, our geographies, and even our place in history make us all different. We are uniquely shaped into who we are. This makes us all diverse, just as diverse as the rest of God's creation. That is the beauty of God's plans.

But how should we view diversity in God's world? Let's think about God's plan of diversity. God gave us dominion over all the creatures of the earth; another term for dominion is "stewardship." What does stewardship mean? Stewardship means being responsible in taking care of things entrusted to our hands. We are given diversity, but as human beings what do we do with it?

How many of you have heard the story of the mongoose in Hawaii?

The mongoose was introduced to Hawaii in the mid-nineteenth century, imported from Jamaica to control the rat population that was destroying the plantation crops. (Rats were imported by the early sailors.) For several reasons, however, this "solution" failed to work. First, the mongooses were active mostly during the day, while rats were active at night. Second, the mongooses ate the native insects, small cats, snakes, frogs, and many of the native birds and their eggs. Third, the female mongooses could produce a litter of two to five pups a year. Lastly, unlike in other places, there were no natural predators of the mongoose in Hawaii. Therefore, when humans interfered and brought in one species to take care of another, the plan backfired, creating havoc in the Hawaiian ecosystem and endangering native species.

The mongoose is just one example of how we human beings have been poor stewards of what God has entrusted into our hands. God created this diversity. The challenge is how do we handle this diversity?

Questions to Ponder . . .

1. Where have you seen God's diversity in the world?
2. What examples of interdependence (relying and depending on each other) and interconnectedness (connecting with each other at different levels) can you cite among God's creation?
3. Why do you think God intentionally made such a diverse world?

4. Where have you seen humanity's interference with God's creation? How was it positive or destructive?
5. As you think about humanity's interdependence and interconnectedness, where do you see them in your daily lives? How are we interconnected and interdependent in our communities? Our own ethnic groups? The nation? Globally?
6. Reflect on the impact one person can make within this interdependence and interconnectedness. Give one or two examples from your own life or community.

CHAPTER 2

Diversity of Human Beings in the Bible

The Bible is full of examples and illustrations of God's relationship with the diversity of human beings. Diversity as expressed in concern for others who are different from us is a dominant biblical theme. Two words that are used throughout the Bible are the Hebrew word *goy* and the Greek word *ethnos* (see the online workbook, chapter 2, "The Word *Goy*" and "*Ethnos* Is an Ethnic Group," for additional information). In fact, these two words are used more often than the words for grace, forgive or forgiveness, faith, pray or prayer, and love.

What does the word *goy* mean? *Goy* is simply a non-Jew, a Gentile. Many Bibles in English have translated this word as "nations" or "peoples." See the following Scriptures for some examples of *goy*: Genesis 22:17-18 (nations); Isaiah 11:10 (peoples); and Zechariah 2:10-11 (nations).

Questions to Ponder . . .

1. How would you define nations or nationality?
2. In some ways, nations are a way to imply who is "in" or "like us" and who is "out" or "unlike us." Thinking back to your childhood and upbringing, how was this defined for you?

3. How were you taught to treat those who are "like us" and those who "aren't like us"?

What about *ethnos*? *Ethnos* simply refers to an ethnic group or ethnic groups. *Ethnos* or an ethnic group is a group of people who self-identify, usually on the basis of common genealogy, ancestry, or similarities of language, history, culture, society, or nation. Ethnicity is not race. Race is another category defined by outsiders, so it is a social construct, usually created by society. On the other hand, ethnicity is self-defined. For example, a person of Asian ancestry, born and raised in Latin America, who speaks only a native Spanish and knows only the local native culture, can decide to define herself or himself as ethnically Hispanic or Latinx. See examples of the English translation "nations" of the Greek *ethnos* (representing ethnic groups) in Matthew 28:18-20; Mark 11:17; Acts 2:1-6; Revelation 7:9-10.

Questions to Ponder . . .

1. To what ethnic group(s) do you belong?

2. In the United States, the question of ethnicity is further complicated by the increasing numbers of "interracial" and "intercultural" marriages. If you were the offspring of such a union, how would you decide to which racial or ethnic group you would belong? What would be your criteria?

3. What is the importance of having an ethnic group(s)? Why do human beings feel the need to identify with an ethnic group?

4. Realizing ethnic groups exist, in what ways can we best relate to one another?

CHAPTER 3

God's Story of Redemption Includes Diversity

So, what is God's plan for the diverse peoples of the world?

First, from the beginning, God's plan of redemption has included people from diverse nations. God's promise to Abraham was that through *his* people (his offspring) all nations would be blessed. God's blessing isn't confined to the immediate descendants of Abraham, or to his own ethnic group. God's blessing is to be shared among all peoples, not just God's original "chosen" people (Genesis 22:17-18). This means that one ethnic group isn't more chosen or more gifted or more rewarded. God's blessing is given to everyone equally. The root of Jesse—the lineage that comes from Jesse, King David's father—will include non-Jews and people of other nations who will embrace the Messiah (Isaiah 11:10). Jew and Gentile will fall under God's banner.

The implication for the church is that one's own cultural expression of Christianity is not superior to another's expression. These expressions are just different. Like God's created world, each expression is a gift from God and is to be celebrated.

Second, God's plan is to adopt all of earth's people into God's family. This will take place at the coming of the Messiah. Then God will call the diverse nations God's people (Zechariah 2:10-11), and all will become God's heirs (see Romans 8:14-19).

Third, God's plan through Jesus Christ is to actively seek out people from diverse nations to tell them God's story of redemption. This is not a passive directive. Jesus calls his disciples to purposely engage with people of diverse nations. It is a call to go beyond our own ethnic groups and seek out relationships with those who are different from us.

Fourth, God's plan is for the Christian church to be inclusive. Mark takes "seeking out diverse peoples" further by saying that Jesus' "house of prayer," the church, is for all nations (Mark 11:17).

Fifth, God's plan is that the church should be diverse in ethnicity and languages. One of the common misconceptions in the church is that the church should be one, interpreted to mean homogeneous, or monocultural. Why do we need different ethnic and language churches? In Acts, the famous passage about Pentecost tells us that the church should be diverse ethnically, with followers who can speak and understand the different languages. All of this is made possible by the Holy Spirit. It is the Holy Spirit who will enable believers to take the time to communicate and relate to the diversity God planned for the church (Acts 2:1-6). This is the unity called for, not unity of language, not unity of culture, not unity of faith expression, not even unity of theological understandings. This unity is based on mutual engagement, respect, and understanding. It is through the Holy Spirit who gives us the desire, the courage, and the power to go beyond our own ethnicity, cultural understanding, and comfort zones that we can be united with others who are very different from us.

Sixth, God's plan is that we respect and honor the diversity of cultures. In Galatians, Paul admonishes Peter (Cephas) for being a hypocrite. Peter was one of the first to reach out to Gentiles to convert them. However, when Peter was among his own people and confronted, he echoed the belief that the Gentiles had to take on some of the Jewish laws in order to be accepted into the church. Peter even avoided being around the Gentiles. Paul accused him of being afraid of what his ethnic church members might say instead of honoring the truth in the gospel. The truth that Paul expressed was that the Gentiles did not have to become ethnic Jews to be accepted into God's church. God would accept them as they were, as Gentile Christians (Galatians 2:11-14).

Christians do not have to "look" like or even "act" like one another to be accepted into God's family. We do not have to have the same traditions or rules in our churches to be part of God's church.

Finally, God's plan is that at the end times, "every nation, tribe, people and language" will be represented in God's restored kingdom. We will be with God, and there will be peace (Revelation 7:9-10).

This is God's ultimate plan. This is God's story.

Questions to Ponder . . .

1. What has been your experience with churches that express their faith differently than your own church?
2. It is said that the most segregated hour in the United States is the hour of the Christian worship service. How do you interpret this statement?
3. How is this a hindrance to Christian unity and relationships among diverse cultures and ethnicities? How can this be seen as a gift?
4. How is your church attempting to be more inclusive? To Christians of different theological perspectives? To believers of other faiths? To agnostics? To atheists?

CHAPTER 4

What the Bible Says About Relating to Diverse Peoples

There are many more biblical passages that teach us about God's desire for us to relate with people who are different from us than those previously mentioned (see Deuteronomy 10:17-19; 24:17-19).

God plainly teaches us to treat the "foreigners" or strangers in our midst with compassion, mercy, and kindness. And God reminds the believers that they were once "foreigners and strangers" themselves.

In a real sense, we Christians are also "foreigners and strangers" in this world. Until we are reunited with God, we are just passing through this world. So, who do we consider foreigners and strangers in our communities and in our nation? Perhaps even in our churches?

Here's an Exercise . . .

On a sheet of blank paper, draw a picture of a "typical American." What features do you want to include? What physical characteristics? What does an average American look like? (See the exercise "Ten Friends" in chapter 4 online.)

Questions to Ponder . . .

1. What gender or ethnic group did you draw?
2. Why did you draw what you did?
3. Had you thought of drawing an American of a different racial or ethnic group? Why or why not?
4. Would you consider someone from another racial/ethnic group to be a foreigner or stranger? Why or why not?

What Jesus Says About Relating to Diverse Peoples

In the New Testament, Jesus teaches and demonstrates even more plainly what we are to believe and do in our relationships with other ethnic and cultural groups (see Matthew 22:35-40; chapter 4, "Discussion of Jesus and the Woman at the Well," online).

The question raised in this passage is, Whom do we define as our neighbor? Obviously, our neighbors are the ones who live near us. We can even expand our definition of neighbor to our extended family. We would even say our friends, our fellow church members, our co-workers, and even our acquaintances from the supermarkets, the gas stations, or the many places we frequent in our daily lives. Does neighbor extend to people we don't know? Would neighbor include the undocumented, the homeless, the prisoners, the people in other countries, the people of other faiths, even the people our country is at war with? What about the bigots and racists?

For Jesus, neighbor is all-encompassing. Remember the story of the Good Samaritan? There are some important key points in that familiar parable to consider or reconsider (see Luke 10:29-37).

First, we know nothing about the man being robbed or the robbers. We don't know their ethnicity. The one being robbed and the robbers could be Jewish or Gentile.

Second, we do know that the priest and the Levite were Jewish and that neither of them helped the victim. Perhaps the victim was a Gentile. That's why they didn't help. To touch and help the Gentile would have been a defilement. And if the victim was Jewish, the priest and Levite's passing by would have been even worse, since they refused to help a fellow Jew. They might have seen this Jewish victim in his present state as also "unclean."

Third, the Samaritan, a member of an ethnic group the Jewish religious leaders considered unclean, was the one who helped and showed compassion and generosity. If the Samaritan helped the victim who was also an "unclean" person, that was great. If the Samaritan helped the victim who was Jewish, that was even more remarkable. Whatever the case, the Samaritan overcame the limits of his own comfort zone and his fear and concerns for his own safety to do what is expected of a decent human being.

Jesus makes the point that everyone is our neighbor, including those whom we fear or despise.

Questions to Ponder . . .

1. Not all "neighbors" are the same. At times there are "bad neighbors" or "neighbors of our worst nightmares." However, in terms of our Christian faith, who are the neighbors we have the most difficulty understanding or getting along with? Why is that? How can we remedy the situation?
2. The Jews had a strong bias and prejudice toward the Samaritans and Samaria. Samaria is a place they would avoid. The area made them uncomfortable; perhaps they

even thought it was a dangerous place. Therefore, the Jews preferred to avoid encounters with the Samaritan people. Do we avoid certain neighborhoods, cities, and places because they make us feel uncomfortable or unsafe? Are we uncomfortable with particular groups of people, and would we rather avoid them? Why do we feel this way?

3. How might we overcome our fears and discomfort in order to go into our Samaria and engage our Samaritans?

CHAPTER 5

The Early Church and Diversity

After Pentecost, the church carried on Jesus' message and grew and expanded, moving farther and farther throughout the Roman Empire. As the church grew, it struggled with how to tell and demonstrate God's story. As more and more cultures and ethnicities were added to its membership, the church had to interpret God's story in new ways. How would the church create meaning and understanding for each new group of people without jeopardizing the truths and principles of faith that already had been established?

Acts 6:1 records one such ethnic-related conflict in the early church between Hellenistic Jews (Greek-cultured) and Hebrew Jews (traditional Jewish-cultured). The Hellenistic Jews complained that their widows were being neglected, while the Hebrew widows were being served. Apparently, the Hebraic leaders, who were in charge in the early church, quickly came up with a solution that involved both the traditional and Hellenistic Jews (see Acts 6:2-7).

The church continued to expand and grow greatly as a result of increased persecution. Sometimes opportunity arises out of crisis. As the church members moved to different locations for survival, they found themselves in the midst of other cultures. Growth began to happen as the demographics changed, and the church found itself needing to adapt and minister to new people groups (see Acts 8:4-5, 14-17, 26-29, 36-38).

Questions to Ponder . . .

1. How has your church reached out to different groups of people?
2. If your church has or has not, what have been the challenges?
3. What did you learn from this experience?
4. What might you try next or do differently?

The Early Church Overcomes Ethnocentrism

Adapting, welcoming, and including other ethnic groups was not an easy process for the early church. It took some soul searching for the early Jewish Christians. Peter was one of the first to begin ministering to foreigners. Peter had been converting Hellenistic Jews, but now he had to be confronted with his own bias and prejudice about all ethnic groups.

God convicted Peter to go to a Gentile and convert his whole household. For Peter to do this, he had to overcome years of upbringing and teaching, his culture and society, his friendships, and his ethnocentrism. Peter had to go outside of his comfort zone and safety net and travel to unknown territory to build relationships with people he thought were unworthy of his friendship. But he did, and the result was the converting of an entire family (see Acts 10:9-20).

God's story can be uncomfortable and frightening. In Acts 11:1-18, we read that Peter's action caused conflict among the churches, and he had to answer to his own church leaders. How dare he do what he did!

As God's story continued, the early church grew in believers, and with growth came additional controversies. New understandings and consensus had to be built along the way. According to Acts 15:1-14, 19-21, one of the major controversies was over circumcision, a requirement for all Jewish males. Would non-Jewish converts need to be circumcised, too? In order to make wise decisions about circumcision and other weighty matters, the early church discovered that it would have to reinterpret what was essential and nonessential to the faith. In other words, the church made an effort to understand the growing diversity of the believers, to respect that, and to adapt (see Acts 15:1-14, 19-21).

This didn't end future challenges as the church continued to become more inclusive. A dispute arose among the Christians in regard to eating meat that had been sacrificed to idols (1 Corinthians 8:4-9). Some Christians thought it was all right, while others were offended by it, so Paul taught that even though what we do is acceptable in our culture or in society and does not affect our salvation or faith, we ought to be aware of how it might cause our fellow Christians to stumble in their faith. In other words, in our diversity we must be aware of how what we do helps or hurts others in their journey of faith.

And finally, Paul taught that in our diversity, unity comes through Christ (Ephesians 2:14-22). It is through Christ that diverse people can come together, barriers can be destroyed, walls of hostility can be torn down, and a new humanity can be forged. Christ, through the Holy Spirit, is the peacemaker. This is God's story (see 1 Corinthians 8:4-9; Ephesians 2:14-22).

Questions to Ponder . . .

1. As you begin the journey to relate to persons of different racial, ethnic, or cultural groups, what are some hurdles that you perceive you might encounter?

PART 2

OUR STORY

Rev. Kathryn Choy-Wong

CHAPTER 6

The History of Racism in the World

Exactly when "racist" attitudes began to appear in world history is unclear. Early indications began around the Middle Ages in Europe, around the fifth century to the late fifteenth century, from the time of the fall of the Roman Empire to the time of the Renaissance. Jews, who became the victims of prejudice and discrimination, were identified as the *devil,* and a concerted effort was made to convert them to Christianity.

During this time Europeans were increasing their contact with people of darker pigmentation from not only Asia but also Africa, and later the Americas and the Pacific Islands. The reason Europeans gave for enslaving Africans was that Africans were heathens. The Christian religion was used to justify their enslavement, with an interpretation of a passage in Genesis maintaining that Ham committed sin against his father, Noah, which then condemned his black descendants to be forever servants.

A "scientific" theory of race began to emerge in addition to the biblical interpretation. Eighteenth-century scholars began to think human beings were subdivided into three to five "races." The three main "races" were Caucasoid (e.g., European, white, and some Hispanic), Mongoloids (e.g., Asians and indigenous peoples), and Negroid (e.g., Africans and some Pacific Islanders). Those who perpetuated slavery even justified it by claiming that these races were separate species of humans.

In the nineteenth century, nationalism and imperialism contributed to intensifying racism in Europe and the United States. Although slavery was eventually abolished, and some reforms were made, racism has never been eradicated. Relationships among the so-called races became more competitive, and they were pitted against each other. Often people who were seen as "other," whether white (e.g., Irish, Italian, Jewish) or people of color were the scapegoats for the ills of society. In Germany, extreme nationalism went beyond color and culminated in anti-Semitism and the Holocaust. Jews were seen as belonging to a different race than the one to which true Germans belonged.

As Western imperialism and the desire for resources and power continued, Asia, Africa, the Pacific Islands, and the Americas became the target of the claim that those of European descent had the right to rule over these territories and its peoples.

Questions to Ponder . . .

Have you taken the hugely popular DNA test that makes it possible to find out about your ancestry? In May 2021, scientists were able to decode our human genes completely. It is my belief that we Americans have often categorized our population into one or more of the five "races": African (black, Negroid), European (white, Caucasian), Asian (East Asian, Southeast Asian, Mongoloid), Oceanian (Pacific Islander), and Native American (Indian/indigenous). See the glossary at the end of the book.

What is your reaction to these true statements?

1. Two people of European descent may be more genetically similar to an Asian person than to each other.
2. We share 99.9 percent of our DNA with each other.

3. The .1 percent of our DNA that is different from others reflects the differences in our environments and other external factors, not basic biology.
4. Our skin color does not influence our intellect.
5. Our skin color does affect how others behave toward us and we toward others.

CHAPTER 7

Assumptions and Sensitivity

We don't see things as they are; we see them as we are.
—Anais Nin

As we embark on our journey to build intercultural relationships, we start with ourselves, and our own stories. We start with our experiences and the realities we face in our communities and in our environment. We also come with worries, fears, hopes, and desires. We come with many assumptions.

One of my fears is that I will make an assumption about something or someone, and not only be proven wrong but also be embarrassed by my assumption. As a guest at a church anniversary banquet, I entered the restaurant and was greeted by a young woman I had not seen in a long time. We embraced each other warmly, and when I noticed her belly, I made a congratulatory remark about her pregnancy. She looked at me in displeasure and said, "I'm not pregnant." With that in mind, I will attempt to identify some assumptions for our work in becoming bridge builders and building a Beloved Community.

Environmental Assumptions

Prejudice, discrimination, racism, and oppression are learned behaviors. (We will explain more about these in another chapter.) Values, attitudes, and behaviors by which we live are passed along to us. Often, we acquire them from preceding generations, from our current family, and from culture and society. We become so conditioned to "our way of thinking" that we may be unaware of the different and subtle ways we do not love other children of God. We pass this thinking on to our children.

Fear sustains oppression. Fear of losing family, friends, careers, or social standing, or even fear of coercion by others, often keeps us from challenging prejudice, discrimination, racism, and oppression. Our silence or denial can reinforce and perpetuate oppression, even if we are not directly involved in the oppression.

Oppression that is caused by prejudice, discrimination, and racism is often subtle and unrecognized by those perpetuating it. When we routinely assume that people are a certain way because of their cultural background, ethnicity, race, or gender, we are stereotyping. Accepting stereotypes at face value is a form of oppression. Oppression is perpetuated when it is socially sanctioned by the dominant religious, social, and political groups of society. When oppression becomes a pervasive part of culture and is accepted as the norm, going unquestioned and uncontested, then we are perpetuating it and may no longer recognize it as oppression.

We often do not recognize our own involvement in and victimization resulting from racism and oppressive behavior. Those of us who are being oppressed or who have been oppressed have internalized many aspects of our oppression without even knowing it. Again, this is the result of years of conditioning. We begin to believe the lies, stereotypes, and misinformation. Some of us begin to hate ourselves, refuse to see "our people" as attractive, or distance ourselves from our people. We think that the dominant culture is superior, and we are ashamed of who we are. This is internalized oppression.

People will resist being prejudiced, racist, or oppressive, or being a victim of such. Many well-intentioned people will try to recognize prejudice, racism, or oppression and find ways to resist oppressing or dominating others. Those who have been victims of oppressive behaviors will try to find ways to resist being oppressed that may include acting out, organizing against oppression, escaping, and isolating (we will look at this more closely in a later chapter).

Oppression, in any form, is destructive to all. Oppression is a lose-lose situation. When a human life is devalued, every life loses its worth. When creation is mismanaged or oppressed, all life suffers together. The oppressor is locked into a life of fear, anger, or hatred of others that deprives them of God's fullness and beauty of all life. The oppressor misses out on the talents, gifts, and the joys that those being oppressed can bring.

Our lives are enhanced when peace, harmony, and love are maintained in society. Human beings will thrive and reach their fullest potential when they live in an environment that meets basic needs, ponders love and support, and fosters hope for the future.

Now, making assumptions regarding others is natural, and it is our way of processing the data that surround us. Often, we make these assumptions based on our first impressions. However, we should not take these first assumptions at face value because things are typically more complex than we assume; also, we can look at what we experience in more than one way (see chapter 7, "Look at the Images," online).

I love baseball. More accurately, I love playing baseball more than watching it. When I was in fifth grade my family moved to South San Francisco, a suburb just south of San Francisco, near the San Francisco airport. I remember after school the kids in the playground would play baseball. Of course, I joined in, but I was picked last to be on a team. The kids didn't know me, I was a girl, and I was short, so no one wanted me on their team. In fact, they joked about my being on their team because their first impression of me led them to assume that I couldn't play. Little did they know that I was one of six girls out of twenty-six first cousins on my mother's side who all played baseball at our family get-togethers. They didn't know that I could catch and hit. They found out, though!

Relationship Assumptions

When we are in tune with God, we are in tune with our neighbors and ourselves. God provides us the power to overcome obstacles. With God's help, we can love one another as God loves us.

A safe and loving environment is needed if people are to be open and honest about themselves. Such an environment needs to be created for people to freely share themselves. Every person needs to feel supported, respected, and cared for regardless of what is stated by others or felt by oneself.

We begin the process of building bridges by first looking inward to discover how we have been shaped to be victims or victimizers by our personal and social contexts. As we become more aware of ourselves and our attitudes and behaviors, we will become more open to listening and supporting those who seem to be different from us.

We have a true desire to build bridges. We assume that those engaged with us in relationships share our desire to build bridges and break down years of conditioning. Any mistakes made in the process are likely unintentional, come from a lack of knowledge, and/or come from the desire to relate.

We are not perfect, and we will make mistakes. We assume that even though we have the best intentions, we will make mistakes along the way. We will learn from these mistakes and will share with one another in love. With the help of the Holy Spirit, we can be honest with and learn from one another.

We can learn to be supportive friends, allies, and advocates. We can trust people's sincerity and expect that they will try their best to understand and be supportive. As relationships develop, we can learn how to be supporters of, allies with, and advocates for one another.

We need to be patient and not expect things to happen more quickly than possible. Building relationships and bridges is a long but worthwhile process. It will take time for us to develop trusting relationships, to break down old biases and attitudes, and to learn how to risk friendships with people who are different from us. (See chapter 7, "Relationship Quotes," online.)

God is at our side. Through the Holy Spirit, we can and will experience God's presence in our intercultural experiences. We are not alone; God, through the Holy Spirit, is our guide.

Intercultural Sensitivity

Proofs of Jesus' Interculturalism

Three proofs that Jesus was Jewish:
He went into his father's business.
He lived at home until the age of thirty-three.
He was sure his mother was a virgin, and his mother was sure he was God.

Three proofs that Jesus was Irish:
He never got married.
He never held a steady job.
His last request was for a drink.

Three proofs that Jesus was Italian:
He talked with his hands.
He had wine with every meal.
He worked in the building trades.

Three proofs that Jesus was a Californian:
He never cut his hair.
He walked around barefoot.
He invented a new religion.

Telling stereotyped jokes is risky, but I hope this one isn't offensive. Jokes aside, sensitivity is important in developing intercultural relationships.

In intercultural ministries, there is often no right or wrong way of seeing or doing things. Sometimes we have to remind ourselves that it is a matter of cultural perspective. Intercultural sensitivity exercises help us to remember that there are different cultural perspectives and to think through our motives for being in intercultural relationships. These suggested exercises challenge us to recall how each person is made in God's own image, how each is uniquely gifted, and how each is a blessing (see chapter 7, "Intercultural Sensitivity Exercises," online).

It is helpful to become familiar with these exercises, put them into your own words, practice them, and make them a natural part of being in intercultural relationships.

CHAPTER 8

Being Intercultural

We, as human beings, all started as babies. The world revolved around us. When we needed our basic needs met, we certainly let others know about it! We were completely narcissistic, expressive, and yet dependent. So, it is our natural inclination to be self-centered.

However, as we grew older, we began noticing others. We learned what it meant to be a part of a family, a community, a tribe, a cultural group, a nation, and a world. This understanding was taught to us, demonstrated to us, pressed upon us, and sometimes even forced upon us. We learned what it meant to live in our society, specifically in the United States. We learned not only through verbal communication but also by observing others. Our worldview, values, desires, and dreams took shape through our personalities, environment, experiences, and place in human history. Those of us in mainstream USA, in other words, white America, learned that we were "normal." We didn't have to think about who we were as a cultural or ethnic group. We were comfortable with our surroundings for the most part. We didn't feel different from what we experienced in the outside world. We seemed to "fit in" with everyone else. The people we saw on television, in movies, on social media, in education, in hospitals, in governmental leadership, and in corporate management looked like us. In the storybooks we read as children, the characters looked like us. We were pretty much comfortable wherever we went. We could blend in and didn't have to stand out if we didn't want to.

People of color were not considered part of the mainstream because we were neither invited nor permitted to become a part. We learned that we were "different," not the "normal" American. We rarely encountered people in mainstream leadership who looked like us. We did not see many people of color in mass media or in mainstream educational institutions and healthcare professions. We didn't always feel comfortable or welcomed into certain neighborhoods and places of business.

Remember the exercise in chapter 4, where you were asked to draw what a "typical American" looks like? If you ask a number of mainstream people to describe what an average American physically looks like, what do you think they will say? Most will probably describe an American who looks like an Anglo-Saxon, a person from one of the northern European countries. They would not describe an Asian American, an Arab American, a Hispanic/Latinx American, a Native American, or even most of the time, an African or black American. Instead, their description could be described as a child's view of America, characterized by self-centeredness, ethnocentrism, and racial or ethnic bias.

My experience in working interculturally is that Asian immigrant clergy and laity often refer to white churches as American churches as distinct from their own church (e.g., Vietnamese church, Chinese church, Korean church), even though all these churches are in America and, therefore, all are American churches. The thinking here is that white equals American and all other churches with the majority of people of color are "other." Quite telling. —Shan

This view of white America has been dominant and the reality for all of the country's history. It is entrenched in our institutions, societal expectations and acceptances, cultural norms, historical references and resources, entertainment establishments and media, and stories we tell about America. Who are we?

The year 2020 was the year of the census. Every ten years America counts the overall population. The census is important because it determines where resources should be allocated and how the citizens and residents should be represented. Over the course of the history of census-taking, the categories of people and what was deemed important have changed. For instance, racial or ethnic categories evolved.

Let's take a quick look at past census categories.

The first census was in 1790.

1790

- Free white males 16 years and older
- Free white males under 16 years old
- White females, other free persons
- Slaves

1890

- White, colored
- Chinese, Japanese
- Indian (indigenous peoples)

1930

- White
- Negro (If mixed, no matter how small a percentage, people were asked to list themselves as "Negro")
- Mexican, Indian (indigenous peoples)
- Chinese, Japanese, Filipino, Hindu, Korean
- "Other race"

2010

- White
- Black/African American/Negro[1]
- American Indian/Alaska Native
- Hispanic Origin (Mexican/Mexican American/Chicano, Puerto Rican, Cuban, other Hispanic/Latino/Spanish origin)
- Asian Indian, Chinese, Japanese, Filipino, Korean, Vietnamese
- Native Hawaiian, Samoan
- Other Asian or Pacific Islander

These past census categories give us insight into what our government considered to be important information, and they help us discern the country's political agenda. For example, when the 2020 census approached, a great debate took place as to whether the questionnaire that would go to everyone should ask if he or she were a citizen. The debate centered on the motive for asking this question and how the answer might be used. For example, a possible motive is to purposely undercount segments of society in order to prevent services to these communities, or to affect representation and the electoral votes in order to remain in power (e.g., redistricting). Another motivation might be an anti-immigrant sentiment. It is interesting to note that there has not been a citizenship question on the census survey going to the majority of Americans since 1950. For seventy years, this was not a priority question because the main concern was to obtain a more accurate count of the people in our country, regardless of their citizenship status. However, in the early years of the census, some racial or ethnic groups were specifically excluded from citizenship, even if they were born in the United States. It wasn't until 1970 that the Census Bureau added a citizenship question on a long form that went out to a smaller number of households. Later, the census added the American Community Survey, conducted every year since 2005. In this survey, citizenship was asked, but this, too, went out to a small number of people. What was important for our government to know? How did our government's categorizing of those living in America change over time?

The question is, Who are we? What makes us American? Is it our ancestry or place of origin? Is it our shared history? Is it language? Is it our common values? Is it our collective understanding? Is it striving for mutual dreams and goals? Is it belief in an ideal country?

Questions to Ponder . . .

1. If you were to travel to another country where there are few Americans, how would you recognize a fellow American?
2. What values do you think Americans have in common with each other? (If you are curious about how your list compares with a generalized list of US or Western values, see appendix 5, "A Comparison of Western and Eastern Values," online.)
3. How might this diversity of people in the United States benefit the country?
4. What additions or refinement of values does this diversity bring?
5. What challenges does it bring?

Being American

Grinnell College, Iowa, conducting a national poll in 2018, asked, "Who is a real American?" The poll found that a substantial minority had a very narrow view of this question. "Real Americans" were those who were born here, who lived in the United States for most of their lives, who were Christian, and who spoke English. Among Republicans, being born here was the most important criterion, but less so among Democrats. If that is the definition of real Americans, why are some Americans of color who meet these criteria still told to "go home"?

What do Americans value? Ninety percent of those polled said treating people equally; 88 percent said taking personal responsibility was a trait of Americans.

Sebastien de la Cruz, who gained national attention and backlash for singing the national anthem during the 2013 NBA finals in a mariachi outfit, said, "Being American is red, white, and blue, and being free. It doesn't matter what language you speak; if you're born in America, you're still American. No matter what you look like, no matter what."

In 2021, *Minari*, an award-winning film, was classified as a foreign film even though it was about America's immigrants and was produced, directed, acted, and filmed in America. The film depicts a Korean American family who moved to Arkansas. In essence it is an American film; however, since most of the dialogue is in Korean, it was classified as a foreign film. Someone asked whether a Native American film with tribal language would be classified as a foreign film. (In 2018, more than 20 percent of Americans spoke a language at home other than English.)

So, what defines an American?

Changing Demographics and Attitudes

The United States is changing. The US Census Bureau projects that by 2045, whites in America will be in the minority.[2] This is already the case in four states (California, Texas, New Mexico, and Hawaii). The greatest diversity will be among the young. For example, the majority of Gen-Z (those born since 2007) are people of color (see chart on p. 35).

How do Americans view these changes?

In 2019, 6,637 adults responded to a national online survey conducted in English and Spanish by the Pew Research Center to determine how Americans viewed the impact of different races and ethnicities on our country's culture. More than six in ten respondents (64 percent) indicated that the impact was positive.

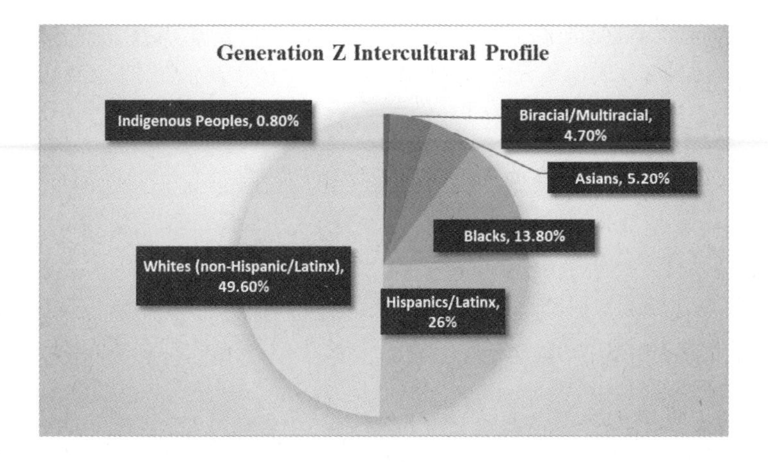

Twelve percent said it was negative, and 23 percent said the presence of different races and ethnicities made no difference. In theory, there was a positive view of diversity, but personal experiences were more limiting. The research found that only one in four white Americans had much interaction with Blacks and Latinx. And half of white Republicans indicated they were bothered by people speaking a foreign language in public. Opinions on these issues also vary considerably along party lines, with Democrats and those who lean to the Democratic Party more likely than Republicans and Republican sympathizers to express positive views of the importance and impact of racial and ethnic diversity. This is the case even after taking into account the differences in the racial composition of the two parties.[3]

In other words, in the abstract, white Americans say they view diversity as positive, but in reality, they have little to do with diverse cultures and lack understanding of and patience with them. In fact, when asked about the prospect of people of color becoming the majority of the US population, which the US Census projects to be inevitable, white Americans' view of diversity becomes negative. In a December 2018, survey conducted by the Pew Research Center, more white Americans said that having a majority nonwhite population would weaken

American customs and values (38 percent) than those who said it would strengthen them (30 percent).[4]

Then who will we consider as Americans? What customs will we retain and what will change? Will we have common values as Americans? For some Americans these questions pose uncertainty, challenge, and anxiety. For other Americans these questions point to a welcoming future.

Questions to Ponder . . .

1. What three to five values do you think are "American" values? What do they mean to you? (See chapter 8, "Values Exercise," online.)
2. Think about one of these values.
3. How do you recognize this value or how do you know someone has this same value? What is shown to you outwardly, verbally, in his or her behavior, or in his or her actions that says, "This person has this same value as I"? In other words, how do you recognize this value in other people?
4. How might this same value be exhibited (outwardly, verbally, behavior, action) in a different way than you are used to, especially in a different cultural context?
5. How might you retain your value but act or behave in a different way in a different cultural context? What would you need to know to be able to do this?

For example, love is a value I cherish, especially with my parents. However, in my Asian American context, my parents' love was not expressed by kissing, hugging, or saying the words "I love you." Instead, parental love was expressed by meeting my physical needs . . . making sure I had food, shelter, money for school, making sure I did my homework. My parents never said they loved me, but

I knew that they did. However, when I worked with children and youth from other cultures, love was still a value, but I expressed it differently from my parents. I gave the children in our church hugs, high fives, and words of praise. I adapted my behavior to fit the cultural context, but love was still my cherished value. —Katie

NOTES

1. Negro was a term used in the US Census prior to 2020.
2. For the chart about Generation Z's intercultural profile: During that year, whites will comprise 49.60 percent of the population in contrast to 26 percent for Hispanics, 13.80 percent for Blacks, 5.20 percent for Asians, and 4.70 percent for biracial/multiracial populations. William H. Frey, "US White Population Declines and Generation 'Z-Plus' Is Minority White, Census Shows," *The Avenue*, Metropolitan Policy Program, Brookings Institute (June 22, 2018), https://www.brookings.edu/blog/the-avenue/2018/06/21/us-white-population-declines-and-generation-z-plus-is-minority-white-census-shows/.
3. These are among the key findings on views about diversity from a nationally representative survey of 6,637 US adults conducted online from January 22 to February 5, 2019, in English and Spanish, using Pew Research Center's American Trends Panel.
4. Kim Parker, Rich Morin, and Juliana Menasce Horowitz, "Looking to the Future, Public Sees an America in Decline on Many Fronts," *Pew Research Center* (March 21, 2019): 1, https://www.pewresearch.org/social-trends/2019/03/21/public-sees-an-america-in-decline-on-many-fronts.

CHAPTER 9

Being a Beloved Community

America is not like a blanket—one piece of unbroken cloth. America is more like a quilt—many patches, many pieces, many colors, many sizes, all woven together by a common thread. —Rev. Jesse Jackson

As Americans, we are changing. We are evolving. We are becoming. America will not be the same America of one hundred years ago or even a decade ago. Change is inevitable. How we accept this change—personally, in our churches, and as a society—is crucial to an America that is living up to its ideals. By doing the hard work of understanding ourselves and being willing to relate interculturally, we are building the concept of a Beloved Community. Rev. Dr. Martin Luther King Jr. had a vision of America becoming the Beloved Community. King expressed it as "the solidarity of the human family." Catching a glimpse of what America could be, after the March to Montgomery in 1966, King said, "As I stood with them and saw white and Negro, nuns and priests, ministers and rabbis, labor organizers, lawyers, doctors, housemaids, and shopworkers brimming with vitality and enjoying a rare comradeship, I knew I was seeing a microcosm of the mankind of the future in this moment of luminous and genuine brotherhood."[1]

To King, a Beloved Community is a community of diverse individuals, in each one's giftedness and glory, interdependent and working together for the common good.

In *Killing Rage, Ending Racism,* author bell hooks describes the Beloved Community as "formed not by the eradication of difference but its affirmation, by each of us claiming the identities and cultural legacies that shape who we are and how we live in the world . . . to form Beloved Community we do not surrender ties to precious origins."[2]

Even the state of Hawaii has something to say about the Beloved Community, having codified it in its legal statutes, calling it the Aloha Spirit (see chapter 9, "Aloha Spirit," online).

Who are we becoming as Americans? Can we embody the Beloved Community? (See chapter 9, "Describe the Beloved Community," online.)

NOTES

1. Kenneth L. Smith and Ira G. Zepp Jr., *Search for the Beloved Community: The Thinking of Martin Luther King Jr.* (Valley Forge, PA: Judson Press, 1998), 132.
2. bell hooks, *Killing Rage, Ending Racism* (New York: Henry Holt and Company, 1996), 265.

PART 3

BEGINNING THE JOURNEY

Dr. Lucia Ann McSpadden

CHAPTER 10

Discovering Each Other's Story Through Our Stories

Looking again at the story of the Good Samaritan, as people of faith, we affirm that God's plan is built on welcoming the stranger, treating the neighbor as ourselves, and caring for the foreigners and groups marginalized by our society (Luke 10:25-37). We are led to recognize that, indeed, "diversity or concern for others who are different from us is a dominant theme of the Bible."

Yet often, we are uneasy as we go beyond words to action. We understand ourselves as good people intending to live a welcoming, inclusive life, and we want our church and community to reflect that value. In spite of this self-identity, however, we frequently struggle with welcoming and including those whom we encounter in our daily lives who are different from us, surprising ourselves when we expect them (miraculously?) to be just like us. How might we understand this contradiction? How can we reconcile our beliefs with our actions? That is our spiritual challenge, and it is not a new challenge.

In this regard, Jesus was uncomfortably clear when he was asked, "Who are my mother and my brothers?" Jesus responded,

"Whoever does the will of God is my brother and sister and mother" (Mark 3:33, 35). This is a call to new relationships, to redefining family, and it wipes out accepted social values. Jesus asserted this claim within a society like ours, in which social boundaries divided people into "us" and "them"; for example, Jews and Samaritans, men and women, our tribe and foreigners. His parable of the Good Samaritan challenges the accepted norm, turning it upside down. He carries on this theme in Matthew 25:31-44 as he refers to persons responding to the needs of the hungry, thirsty, homeless strangers, the poor, the sick, and those in prison in "all the nations," asserting forcefully, "Truly I tell you, just as you did it to one of the least of these who are members of my family, you did it unto me" (Matthew 25:39-40). Jesus was certainly counter-cultural! He redefined our relationships as gospel-shaped: instead of being brothers and sisters by birth, Jesus has called us to be brothers and sisters by choice—to be family.[1] We follow Jesus when we embrace those who are different from us, welcoming their life experiences and insights, knowing that our lives will be enriched and more connected to reality. This is one way we can "walk our talk."

As we jump into this arena, the very human challenge is the tendency to think of "us and them." Wearing blinders to shield us from those who are different in some important way can be a knee-jerk response. Sometimes we are not even clear about why we react in a defensive way. Such an almost automatic reaction is not a mark of a "bad" person; it is a non-reflective, often natural reaction. So, one might ask, "Is there any hope for becoming open and more welcoming of difference?"

Thankfully, we are not left wandering in the wilderness. When we commit ourselves to engage this gospel challenge, we can gain self-understanding and active skills leading to deeper relationships across differences. Our lives thereby expand, and we become increasingly self-reflective and engaging as we develop interactive skills to build connections and trust. It may surprise you that the foundational skill for building such relationships is understanding ourselves, our culture-shaped values, and the messages we have incorporated telling us how to be a "good person." Becoming aware of these cultural, learned values and behaviors will allow us to understand better that our "natural" behavior is not natural but is specific to our cultural group.

It is the aim of this part, "Beginning the Journey," to provide you with guides and markers as building blocks for a deeper understanding, and effective skills leading to a clearer vision and willingness to risk. Take courage, and join the journey. (See chapter 10, "Who Am I? Who Are We? Five Circles of Identity," for an expanded discussion version of the chart below.)

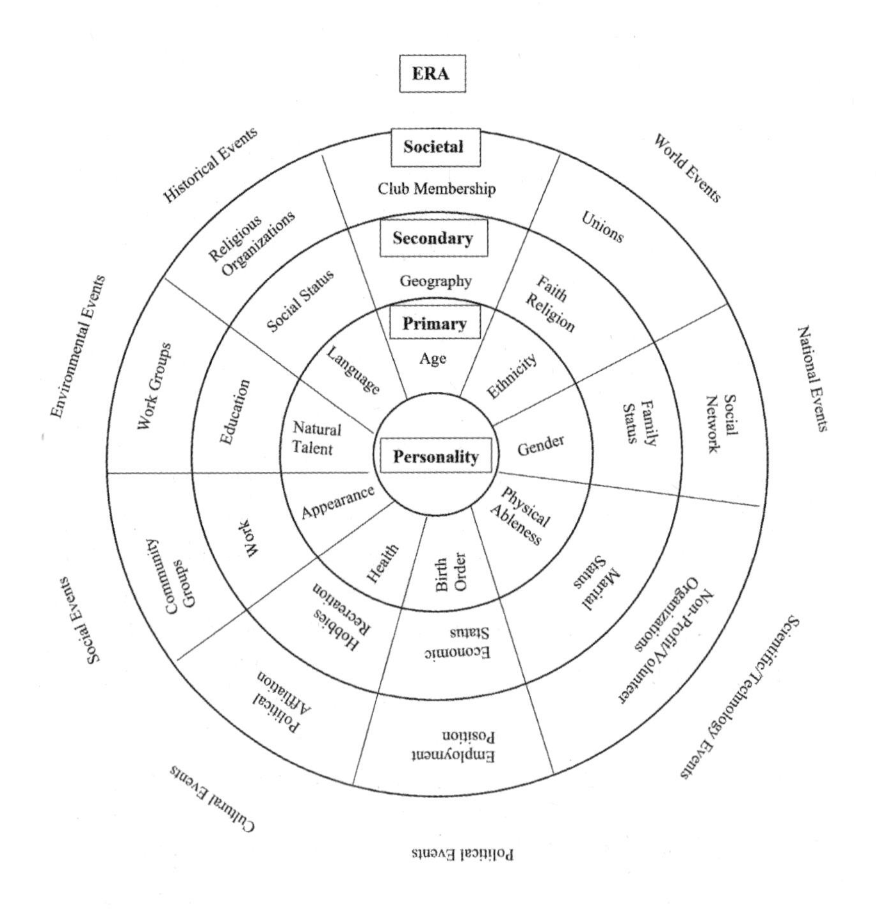

Questions to Ponder . . .

1. Which dimension has had the most influence on you today?
2. Of these dimensions, which one has the most influence on you in the way you view the world and people from other cultures?
3. Of these dimensions, which one has affected your attitude and actions toward people who are different from you? In what way?

NOTES

1. For an in-depth exploration of this theme, see Archie Smith Jr. and Ursula Riedel-Pfaefflin, *Siblings by Choice: Race, Gender and Violence* (St. Louis, MO: Chalice, 2004).

CHAPTER 11

Where Do We Start?

The world in which you were born is just one model of reality. Other cultures are not failed attempts at being you: they are unique manifestations of the human spirit.[1]

You are generalizing, and I don't like that! I am an individual; I feel as if you are labeling me. What do you mean saying "we Euro-Americans"? I'm offended that you are dividing us into different ethnic groups![2]

When we bridge builders were first hit by this passionate pushback, Katie, Dale, and I were taken aback because we assumed that talking about culture was an easy first step in intercultural communication training. How mistaken we were! We realized that we needed to anticipate and engage this strong response if we were to have effective training. Perhaps you also sense some uneasiness and feel labeled when hearing that you are part of a particular cultural group. It seems that "cultural identity" challenges the deep value of individualism in the US. One current expression of this is the negative reaction of many white persons to the Black Lives Matter movement, as revealed in the pushback of "All Lives Matter," although nobody said that they didn't.

Being Human

Katie, Dale, and I struggled to find an effective way to make clear what we meant by culture and cultural groups. We realized that we needed to focus on the universal basics of being human. Intuitively, we all realize, consciously or unconsciously, that our identity and our behavior are shaped by a complex interaction of influences.

Universal qualities: In some ways we are like everyone else in the world—we all have red blood cells; we all need oxygen; we have the same basic survival, physical, and psychological needs.

Cultural influences: We are like some people and not like some other people. We can recognize what a particular group of people have in common with one another and how they are different from every other group (e.g., Tongans have different customs and beliefs than Swedes or people in different regions of the United States).

Personal qualities: Each of us is different from everyone else, including those in our group. Even twins are different from one another. We are wonderfully and individually unique human beings as illustrated in the circles of identity (see chapter 10).

To visualize this, the following model is useful.[3]

Three Aspects of a Person

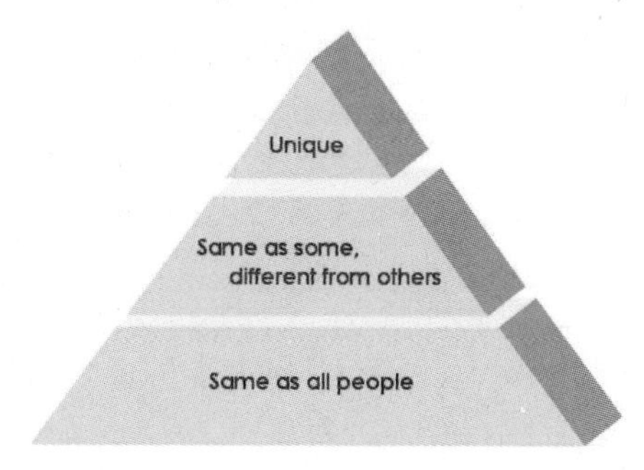

"Culture is the means by which we [express] our identities and establish . . .social belonging and difference." – John Hartigan, Jr.

There are many and various ways of defining or explaining culture. For example:

> Culture is all the learned ways of life of a group of people.
>
> Culture is the shared set of assumptions, values, and beliefs of a group of people by which they organize their common life.
>
> Culture is the way we do things around here!

The most basic way to understand culture is by exploring these questions: Who am I? What group(s) do I belong to where people understand and value me, where I don't feel different, where I know how to act? The following quote states this succinctly: "Culture is the means by which we [express] our identities and establish . . . social belonging and difference."[4] (See chapter 11, "The Mirror," online.)

As we grow into adulthood, we are given many messages. Sometimes these messages are given by family, peers, society, and the media. Sometimes these messages are so deeply internalized that we don't even know they exist until an incident or crisis happens. We just aren't aware of how these messages have influenced us.

When we try to relate to others in an intercultural setting, it is important to know ourselves, how we have been shaped by these messages, and how we act on these messages, consciously or subconsciously. This is where implicit or unconscious bias comes in. We will explore this in more detail in later chapters.

Sometimes, we react to other cultures based on these internalized messages. Be conscious of these messages. What are some clues that we may be having an incident of implicit or unconscious bias? Often, these clues are emotional and physical . . . frustration, anger, sudden anxiety, stomach tied in knots, tensing of muscles, headaches, blushing. What are your signals? (See chapter 11, "Wearing Cultural Lenses" and "Dimensions to Explore," online.)

NOTES

1. Wade Davis, Explorer in Residence, National Geographic, accessed from Syracuse Cultural Workers.com (n.d.) and a Wade Davis, "Dreams from Endangered Cultures," TED talk (February 2003).

2. A participant in an intercultural workshop.

3. The model "Three Aspects of a Person" is adapted from a graph by Chris Smit, Culture Matters, https://culturematters.com.

4. John Hartigan Jr., *Race in the Twenty-first Century: Ethnographic Approaches* (New York: Oxford University Press, 2010), ix.

CHAPTER 12

Ethnocentrism

Let's continue to imagine that you have that very specific pair of glasses with a prescription that has all of these particular learned social expectations ground in (see below image). This prescription leads you to quickly make judgments based on your worldview about other people's beliefs and behaviors. We, as human beings, believe that our reality is the correct way to see the world. However, obviously other people have different glasses with dif-

Ethnocentric Beings[1]

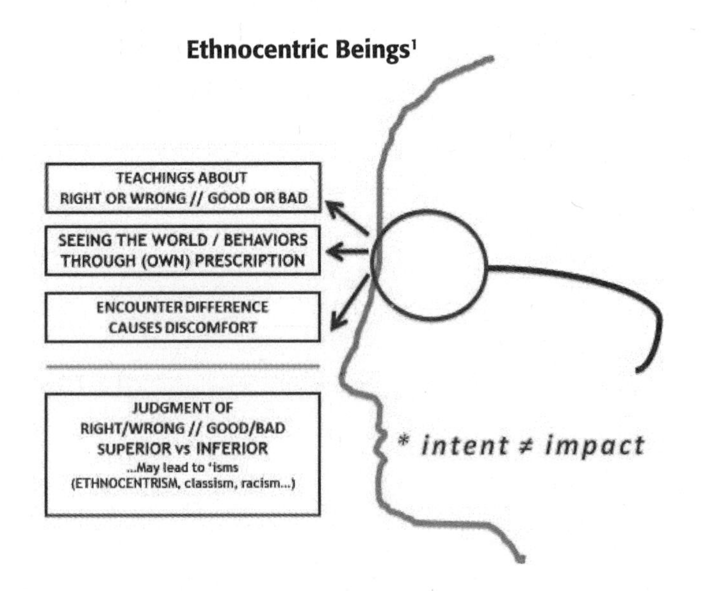

ferent ethnocentric prescriptions.[2] As you look out onto the world and relate to others, this prescription shapes your reactions. If what you experience is what you expect, you likely don't notice anything; your vision is clear, all is "normal." However, when other people have a different prescription from yours, their actions may make you uncomfortable; they are not acting "normal" or "right" according to your prescription. When this happens, you are assuming that those persons are operating within the values of your own cultural context (see chapter 12, "Different Cultural Contexts," online). But they are not! We are likely to have a different, immediate, uneasy, almost unconscious reaction. The following quotes from Albert Einstein rather sharply summarize the challenges:

> Common sense is nothing more than a deposit of prejudices laid down in the mind before you reach eighteen.[3]
>
> It is harder to crack a prejudice than an atom![4]

Before we go any further, it is important to remember that all persons develop prejudices because all persons grow up with a particular set of cultural and social expectations of appropriate behavior. All persons have special prescription glasses.

NOTES

1. This image was developed by our i-Relate colleague Rev. Sun Hee Kim.
2. For a further discussion see *Meeting God at the Boundaries: A Manual for Church Leaders*, Lucia Ann McSpadden (Nashville: The General Board of Higher Education and Ministry, The United Methodist Church, 2006), 26ff.
3. Lincoln Barnett, The Universe and Dr. Einstein (Mineola, NY: Dover Publications, 1948).
4. Broadly attributed to Albert Einstein.

CHAPTER 13

Assessing Difference

Culture (and individuals within cultures) is like an onion—there are many layers. Keep peeling the layers away so you understand more and more. Do not let stereotypes rule your thinking.

Prejudices often develop into strongly held stereotypes. Stereotypes are simplistic. They are ways we attempt to label a group to bring order to a large amount of information and perceptions we have gathered about that particular group of people. They are based on some semblance of reality. However, stereotypes are formed from outside of the group and persons in question and can develop even if we have had no personal experience with a particular group of people. I was surprised, living in Montana, when I met many persons who had never met a black American but had strong stereotypes about black people. These stereotypes are persistent and imply that how a given group of people believe and behave is predictable and the same for all members of that group.

A personal example: When I was thirteen, my family moved from Michigan to Los Angeles. Of course, we had to find a place to live. As a family we looked at various houses; one I particularly liked because it had bright tiles, which I had never seen. I said to my dad, "Oh, I think we should get this house!" My dad's response was, "No, there are too many Norwegians in this neighborhood!"

This was a personal prejudice leading to a stereotype that led to my father acting to avoid a particular group of people. In this case, the response ended there. However, when prejudice is enforced by power and the personal becomes socially embedded, it becomes an "ism." "Isms" develop when we use our influence, power, and privilege to favor our group and create a negative reality for others based on specific identities, for example, gender or race. Keeping with this example, had my father had a major influence in a community, he might have been able to instigate zoning regulations that would have prevented Norwegians from buying and/or renting in that community. It is interesting to note that, to my knowledge, my father had never had any interaction with Norwegians. Where did his stereotype come from?

This is precisely what has happened many times in the US as specific groups of people have been prevented from living in a given community. I lived in San Francisco, where early in the twentieth century, Chinese people were not allowed to live anywhere except in Chinatown. Chinese children were not even allowed to attend public schools. Glendale, California, where I lived as a teenager, was (unbeknownst to me at the time) a "sundown town," which meant that black Americans had to be out of town before sundown.

Living in Mexico and later in Sweden, I was the recipient of some stereotypes. Usually, the perception began with something like, "I know you must have a lot of money because all Americans are so wealthy." Or "You have to be careful the way you treat staff here at the Institute because you Americans are so hierarchical in dealing with others." My colleagues, Dale and Katie, undoubtedly have been labeled with social stereotypes, too.

When I worked for our denomination's national staff, I would travel to parts of the United States where there were few Asians.

Two questions I received often were, "Where did you learn English so well?" and "Where did you come from?" To the second question I would answer, "I am from San Francisco." They would then ask, "No, before that?" I would answer "San Francisco." "No, where were you born?" I would answer, "San Francisco."

They would reply, "No, before that!" These questions all implied that I could not possibly be born in the United States, nor could I be a real American. Never mind that my mother was also born in the United States and Chinese Americans have been in this country since the 1800s. The implication that Asian Americans are forever foreigners means that they can never be accepted as part of and contributors to this country. —Katie

As people of faith, our spiritual challenge is to become more self-aware of our beliefs and values and recognize that these are shaped by how we were socialized. Our beliefs and values are embedded in our families and in the institutions that nurtured and trained us as we grew up. They are part of who we are, of our identities. However, typically most of this is not in our active consciousness and can lead to unconscious or implicit biases. (We will return to this later.)

An important counter to succumbing to stereotypes is, first, to question them. For example, ask yourself, "What personal experience of mine reinforces or counters this description?" Second, if you have not had any personal experience, become more sharply aware of the messages that you are currently receiving that promote stereotypes, for example, in movies, on television, on news programs, and in discussions with others. Finally, and perhaps most importantly, take the approach of generalizations to shape thinking. We all know how we resent it when someone labels us as the same as other people; for example, "It's scary being on the freeway with you women drivers! You are so erratic!" Or as a neighbor said to me about my bi-racial toddler son, "It will be great to have an athlete in your family. Black boys are so good at sports."

Shaping our assessments of others using a generalization analysis (approach?) would sound something like, "Based on my experience, there is a tendency for Mexican men to have a deep sense of responsibility for the well-being of their families." Or, "It seems from my teaching experience with high school boys that many feel pressured to be tough and strong." In these examples, the assessment or description is tentative and not all-encompassing. It leaves open the likelihood that some boys do not experience this or that some Mexican men have little or no sense of family responsibility. In other words, generalizations acknowledge that there is variation within a specific group of humans (see chapter 13, "The Danger of a Single Story," "Shredding Stereotypes," and "Reflect on Your Own Socialization," online). Groups cannot and must not be painted with one brush! Chimamanda Ngozi Adichie succinctly presents the spiritual challenge for us: "Stereotypes rob people of their dignity."[1]

NOTES

1. Chimamanda Ngozi Adichie, speech at Harvard class of 2018 graduation, May 23, 2018, https://www.youtube.com/watch?v=hrAAEMFAG9E.

CHAPTER 14

Seen and Unseen

Our Hidden Values

We have stressed that much of our cultural values and expectations come from our subconscious. The often-used image of the iceberg is one way to capture the reality that only a small part of our cultural identity, our values, rises to the level of our consciousness (c. 15 percent) in the same way that only a small percentage of an iceberg is visible above the waterline. Most of our values and the beliefs that arise from them are hidden from our own consciousness (c. 85 percent). They are out of our view, "below our waterline."

The RMS Titanic *was sunk by an iceberg. On average only 10 percent of an iceberg is above the waterline.*

It is stunning to realize all these important values, these cultural expectations of ourselves and of others, lie outside of our consciousness—it is breathtaking! Take a moment to let these matters sink into your brain, into your heart. Think about how they shape and give meaning to your life, especially in relationships (see chapter 14, "Iceberg Culture,"[2] online).

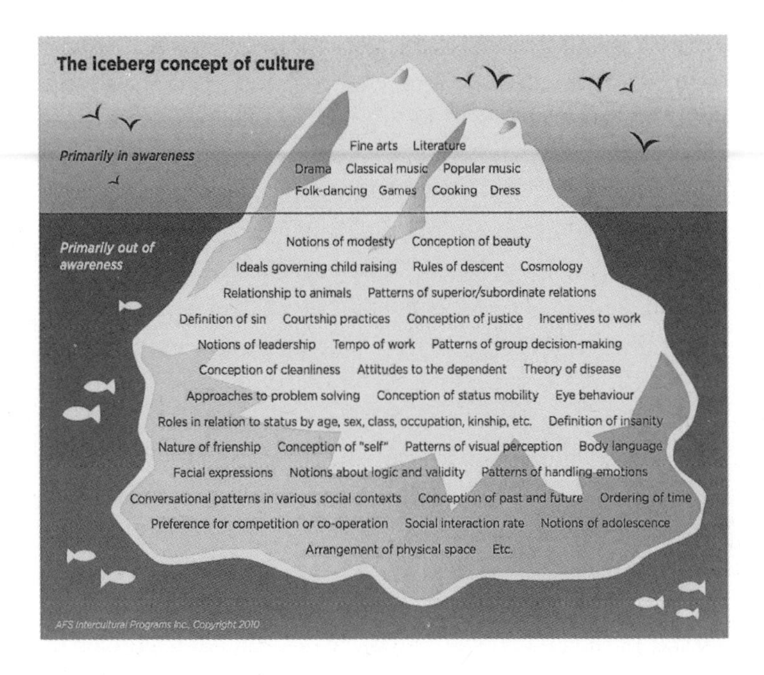

As a child, were you ever told by an adult or a parent, "Look at me when I talk to you!" with the implication that you might be lying or showing disrespect? I was told this over and over again by my father. However, in Asian culture, I would more than likely be taught as a child to avert my eyes when an adult speaks with me. This would be a sign of respect. Having grown up in a very different social environment, an African American elder attending an intercultural workshop stated, "I learned as a child never to look a white person in the eye because it could be understood as a challenge and, therefore, it would be very dangerous."

What did you absorb about how far you, as an adult, should stand from another person who is not a good friend or family member? As an Afghan man comes very close to you, what is your reaction when you hear him ask, "How can I know you if I can't smell you?"[1]

Regarding the iceberg analogy, it can be said that people have their individual icebergs and, like you and me, they are not aware of how much is hidden below their waterline. Imagine good, caring people wanting to develop positive relationships with others who have different cultural icebergs. Surely, at a minimum, being more aware of our "below the waterline" values, our expectations, and the meaning that we attach to behavior will be critical. Again, we are back to the importance of self-awareness, the importance of being willing to let go of judgment and explore meaning. We don't want our different icebergs to crash into one another; we don't want these significant relationships to self-destruct or sink. When, in an intercultural engagement, we are uncomfortable, when we are feeling anxious or stressed, or when we have negative thoughts or judgments, we are likely having an iceberg experience. Remember, the *Titanic* was sunk by an iceberg hidden below the waterline, outside of the captain's awareness. If we want intercultural relationships to be positive, build trust, and caring, we have to lower our own waterline.

All may seem calm above the waterline . . . but cultural icebergs are colliding underneath.

Living and working in Sweden presented me with many iceberg experiences, often happening when I thought I was behaving naturally and kindly. One in particular stands out because it taught me so much. To set the context, it is important to know that in the Swedish workplace, people are not expected nor asked to stay later than the closing time. They are quite precise about this. Therefore, I would never ask Lena, who worked closely with me, to stay late to finish a project.

One time we were working under a timeline to complete a funding proposal. When it came time for Lena to go home, she stayed and we completed the proposal. I was so surprised and touched since this was a gift on her part. The next day we had a staff meeting; I felt moved to share how significant Lena's contribution was to completing the proposal (a very American value of individual recognition). As I reported this, the room became startlingly silent; people looked uncomfortable. Lena looked like she wanted to slide under the table and disappear.

I was uneasy and couldn't understand what I had done. Thankfully, one of my colleagues said calmly, "We wouldn't do that in Sweden." I responded, "Do what?" He then explained that in Sweden one does not bring attention to an individual; contributions from everyone in the group are necessary to accomplish a task. It is a community effort. I asked then how one recognizes and appreciates the special contribution of someone. The response was, "We say *Inte så dum* (not too bad)."[3] Confused, I said, "But that is an insult!" One of my colleagues was a Canadian married to a Swede. She clarified that in English, "not too bad" is an insult, but in Swedish, it is a compliment.

What ensued was a lively, spontaneous, and enlightening discussion. Everyone offered his or her understanding of this deep, under-the-waterline, Swedish worldview that values community over the individual. The atmosphere became positive, with a variety of insights and some laughs. This relaxed sense continued for the four-plus years that I worked there. Sometimes, when I was focused on a task, a person with a sparkling smile would tap me on the shoulder and say, "Not too bad."

Questions to Ponder . . .

1. Identify the positive behaviors that prevented my blunder from becoming a negative and/or destructive experience.
2. How did these behaviors encourage ongoing positive relationships? Be as specific as you can. Discuss this with another person or in a group if you have the opportunity.
3. Based on this example, develop and write down your personal guide for respectfully entering into intercultural discussions. Discuss this guide with another person if possible.

The Swedish experience turned out well. In fact, it deepened our group's relationships in a fun way! However, it could have turned out very differently. When a group like my Swedish colleagues unthinkingly accepts an initial negative reaction to an "outsider's" cultural blunder, a limiting or negative stereotype may develop of that person's cultural or ethnic group, as well as a negative opinion that he or she isn't "acting right." The dominant or "normal-acting" group absorbs a single story about that person or group rather than a complex understanding. If the dominant group doesn't self-reflect and challenge this assumption, it will not be surprising to find that its members will act on the assumption. To make matters even worse, they might avoid a person or a group of people; they might share their negative assessment with friends and colleagues; if the "normal" group has the opportunity or the social power, its members might actively discriminate. For example, as people's résumés are being evaluated for a possible position in a company and the previous "offending" person was a Mexican, the next Mexican who applies for a position might be evaluated in a biased way such as, "Oh, I don't think Manuel would be a good person for the position we are hiring for; you know, he likely won't keep to a schedule and will always want more time to finish an assignment."

Additional Questions to Ponder . . .

1. How do you know you are in a cultural iceberg clash? What are some of the signs or signals that you might get from others?
2. What are some signs or signals you might get from your own reactions and responses, including your physical reactions, such as getting flushed, tying your stomach in knots, finding it hard to breathe, or having your muscles tense up?

3. The *spiritual challenge of intercultural relationships is to be aware of our own cultural iceberg,* and how it shapes our understanding, behavior, and relationships. What are some ways that will help you to see things more clearly and lower your waterline? How could you be more aware and understand others' icebergs, and how their icebergs have affected, impacted, and shaped them without being judgmental?
4. How can you adapt your perspective and change your behavior to build a better relationship with others, keeping your and their icebergs in mind?[4]

NOTES

1. Shared with me by an Afghan refugee.

2. The diagram of the iceberg concept of culture is from AFS Intercultural Programs, Inc., 2010, http://ConceptsandTheoriesofCultureforAFS_Friends.pdf (d22dvihj4pfop3.cloudfront.net).

3. This is the phrase used in Uppsala. In other parts of Sweden, one might say *Inte så dåligt* to mean the same thing.

4. Cultural competency and cultural humility are understood as the ability to adapt one's perspective and the willingness to change one's behavior in order to build a trusting relationship.

CHAPTER 15

Unconscious or Implicit Bias

You may throw up your hands and say, "What is the use if all these different and confusing behaviors and beliefs are so natural to each person! What can we do?" That is precisely the right question and a spiritual question if we truly want to build bridges to connect across differences. This is not hopeless. It does require an active commitment to ongoing self-awareness and self-reflection—precisely goals of spiritual growth—and a willingness upon reflection to adapt our behavior and the thinking that shapes our behavior. This is, as is most spiritual deepening, a lifelong, life-changing, engaging, and joy-filled adventure. We will continue to explore specific ways that will guide us in this task.

Let's start with implicit biases. The speed with which our subconscious takes in information is amazing,[1] and how the subconscious acts so much faster than our conscious mind is beyond comprehension. Implicit biases demonstrate this phenomenon because they differ from suppressed thoughts that a person may conceal for social acceptance; instead, implicit biases are powerful because they are activated involuntarily and beyond a person's awareness or intentional control.[2]

Perhaps surprisingly, implicit biases may be significantly different from our conscious values. I was taken aback when I experienced this in myself. I have lived and worked internationally, and I believed I was a flexible, non-judgmental person. One day, I was waiting to board a bus in San Francisco's Chinatown, along with everyone else lining up and waiting. However, when the bus arrived, the line broke and all the people broke out of line and rushed to the door. I was immediately furious, and the thought erupted in my head, "This is my country, and you must do it our way!" I was horrified and ashamed of myself for this thought that was so opposite of what kind of person I believed I was. (When I lived in Japan, this lining up and then breaking and rushing was precisely the behavior in the train stations. I didn't get angry there; I was somewhat amused, and I strategized how to handle this so I could get on the train in time.)

As an outgrowth of brain research, an increasing awareness of implicit bias in all human beings raises concerns about its effect on our day-to-day interactions and relationships.[3] How significant the effect of implicit bias can be is noted by both a scientist and a well-known US Supreme Court judge. For example, Dr. Nancy Hopkins commented, "If you asked me to name the greatest discoveries of the past fifty years, alongside things like the internet and the Higgs particle, I would include the discovery of unconscious biases and the extent to which stereotypes about gender, race, sexual orientation, socioeconomic status, and age deprive people of equal opportunity in the workplace and equal justice in society."[4]

US Supreme Court Justice Ruth Bader Ginsburg asserted that implicit bias is an aspect of the discrimination many women face. Recognizing that the discrimination women face is more subtle now than the overt discrimination of the past, Ginsburg declared, "Rooting out unconscious bias is much harder."[5]

Implicit biases can be positive as well; unfortunately, however, if the bias is negative and not acknowledged, but rather is taken at face value, the power can be destructive. For example, at a personal level, possible relationships don't happen and/or prejudices are hardened (see the cartoon below).[6] The issue of implicit bias becomes especially important when persons and institutions have legal, social, and economic power that can affect a person's access to society's resources or safety—for example, teachers, police, coaches, pastors, judges, prosecutors, and employers. The Black Lives Matter movement is a response to the often dangerous use of power by the police in regard to the black community, a power perceived to be impelled by both implicit and explicit racial biases.

The danger of unexamined implicit bias came sharply into focus for me when I was a new high school biology teacher with approximately 150 students each day. I became aware that on the first day of class I experienced a negative gut reaction to some of the students. I did not know them; I had never interacted with them. This negative reaction was strong enough that I was nonplussed and concerned. I realized that if I ignored my reaction, I might treat these students differently, and I became somewhat fearful of the possible consequences. What if I acted on these negative feelings that came from out of nowhere? I had almost total power in the classroom, so I made the commitment to be extra aware of my behavior. By the end of the first semester many of these students were such a positive, contributing presence that I looked forward to seeing them each day. I breathed a sigh of relief!

Recently, I have noticed the power of implicit bias regarding my granddaughter's school experience. She is a bright, lively, talented twelve-year-old black girl; however, she is dyslexic, and reading is a major challenge for her. Her mother noted that the child's challenges have often been dismissed by her teachers as a behavioral problem—"She is lazy or doesn't really try"—though the opposite is true; she is eager to learn and to achieve. She takes her schoolwork seriously and is often frustrated. In confronting this perception at a parent-teacher conference, her mother has had to be firm: "Stop, I am not what you seem to believe! Her father and I are very involved in her education and take her achievement very seriously!" The teachers' and principal's unspoken message declared that they were acting out of a negative stereotype that black families are unconcerned and uninvolved in their children's educational pursuits.

Again, it is important to recognize that all persons develop implicit biases. This is a natural outgrowth of our socialization and our experiences, especially those shaped by our age, gender, ethnicity, and social or economic status, as well as the times in which we have grown up and continue to live (our circles of identity). For example, persons who were young adults during the Great Depression would likely have implicit biases shaped by those dire circumstances. I am a native-born, highly educated, Euro-American woman; my life experiences are majorly different from those of my son-in-law, who grew up in Mexico and, due to the death of his parents, wasn't able to attend school and learn to read. Without question, we look at the world through dramatically different glasses.

Questions to Ponder . . .

1. Think about times when implicit bias popped up in you. What were the situations? What did you think? Did these experiences surprise you? Confuse you? Seem to be correctly assessed?

2. As you reflect on these experiences, where do you think these biases came from? Where/how did you absorb them?
3. How have these implicit biases affected your thinking or behavior? If they haven't, why do you think that is true?

"I'm always amazed when people walk up to me and say, 'I'm a Christian,'" she said in 2011, on the occasion of her being awarded the Presidential Medal of Freedom. "I think, 'Already? You already got it?' I'm working at it, which means that I try to be as kind and fair and generous and respectful and courteous to every human being."[7] *—Maya Angelou*

Managing Implicit Biases So They Don't Manage You

Although we can't just wish away our implicit biases, we can manage them like a lion trainer does. When biases pop up, take a deep breath, notice the bias, and decide what to do with it. If you realize that it is not congruent with your basic values, acknowledge that it is there and that you won't be guided by it. "Down and back in your corner!" By doing this, the power of the implicit bias is stripped away. It may show up at times; when it does, notice it and determine whether you will allow it to guide your actions. Perhaps it will even help to sigh a bit and say to yourself, "Here you are again. I told you to go away!"

Having implicit biases does not make you or me a "bad" person. It is yet again a sign that we are human and, in this way, like everyone else. It does, however, require that we be self-aware if we don't want these unconscious biases to control our behavior. "It is probably not possible for us to get rid of all our biases, nor is it desirable. Our brain's way of sorting through lots of stimuli quickly is what allows us to move through the world and survive. What we need to learn is how to slow down the biases that betray our values long enough for us to act in a way that is more aligned with what we believe."[8]

"Growing up, I decided, a long time ago, I wouldn't accept any manmade differences between human beings, differences made at somebody else's insistence or someone else's whim or convenience."[9]
—Maya Angelou

That confronting our implicit biases is a necessary spiritual and emotional challenge does not mean it is an easy one. One of my colleague's experiences illustrates the challenge. She grew up in India after its partition into India and Pakistan. She was taught that Pakistanis hated Indians and that she should be afraid of them and avoid them whenever possible. Otherwise, she would be in a dangerous, life-threatening situation. Later, living and working in California, she took a taxi from the airport to her home. While chatting with the driver, who spoke her language and looked like he came from India as well, she realized that, in fact, he was a Pakistani. She became immediately tense and suspicious, with a tightness in her gut. She searched the back seat of the taxi to see if she had a way to protect herself. She knew she had to figure out how to get out of the taxi quickly. Fear overtook her.

As her agitation increased, she started deep breathing to calm herself and process the situation: the man seemed friendly; he was not in any way threatening her; he was driving her to her home, chatting and in good humor. She continued to reflect on her reactions, and realizing that they were not based on fact, she relaxed and continued her conversation with the driver, arriving home safely and in good time. She continues to process her intense reaction, her implicit bias.[10]

Relating this to implicit bias, if we are engaged in an interaction or even just observing people in a group, we easily do not "see" behavior or "hear" information that we do not expect (See chapter 15, "Review of the Media and Entertainment Arts" and "Did You See It?", online). We analyze what is happening from our expectations often based in our unconscious or implicit biases. For example, I might not see a delightful engagement with a person who interjects comments while I am talking because I expect to experience someone waiting quietly to speak after I finish what I want to say. I find it important to realize that implicit bias includes focusing on one behavior or issue and missing what is, in fact, going on. This happens so easily in intercultural experiences.

We all have implicit bias; we can't help it. There are circumstances that can increase our implicit bias, even when we don't realize it. We have seen evidence of this in the case of law enforcement when quick decisions under pressure need to be made, which too often lead to dire circumstances and misjudgments. The following circumstances can increase implicit bias: lack of sleep, stress, time pressure, multi-tasking, unclear boundaries, lack of decision-making criteria, incomplete information, lack of familiarity with a particular group of people, and heightened emotions such as fear or anxiety, peer pressure, and social or media influence. And things that do not help in dealing with implicit bias are good intentions, avoiding a group of people, anyone telling you to "just reduce bias, or stop being biased," and not believing you have implicit bias.

Again, strategies to deal with implicit bias are similar to the lion tamer. Counteract the circumstances that encourage implicit bias to surface. Be aware of your own emotional and health needs. Be sensitive to your implicit biases when they do appear. Ask yourself the questions in the intercultural sensitivity exercises online. Honestly look at your stereotypes (e.g., chapter 15, "Test Your Implicit Bias," online). Individualize the people within a group. See them in their humanness. Look for opportunities to relate to people in the groups toward which you are biased. Take a deep breath and rethink.

NOTES

1. The subconscious mind can process 20,000,000 bits of info per second. The conscious mind can only process 40 bits of info/sec., so the subconscious mind can process 500,000 times more than the conscious mind. Another take: only about 0.01 percent of all the brain's activity is experienced consciously. http://kirwaninstitute.osu.edu/wp-content/uploads/2015/05/2015-kirwan-implicit-bias.pdf.

2. The subconscious is powerful because it controls what we think of ourselves, others, the world, our system of beliefs, and how our life works (our self-image, the lifestyle we "deserve," and all things we think we can or can't do).

3. See the detailed report on implicit bias from the Kirwan Institute, http://kirwaninstitute.osu.edu/wp-content/uploads/2015/05/2015-kirwan-implicit-bias.pdf.

4. Dr. Nancy Hopkins, "Invisible Barriers and Social Change," from the 141st Commencement Baccalaureate Address at Boston University, May 18, 2014.

5. Quoted in "State of the Science: Implicit Bias Review" (Columbus, OH: Kirwan Institute for the Study of Race and Ethnicity, 2015), 1.

6. The cartoon is from www.evanscartoons.com.

7. Maya Angelou, as quoted from "Culture at Large: The unassuming faith of Maya Angelou" by Kimberly Davis, May 29, 2014, *Think Christian*, https://thinkchristian.net/the-unassuming-faith-of-maya-angelou.

8. V. Myers, "He's Black. What Do You Mean He Can't Dance? Check for Your Biases When Things Get Bumpy," *GPSolo eReport* 2, no. 1 (2012), http://www.americanbar.org/publications/gpsolo_ereport/2012/august_2012/ check_biases_1when_things_get_bumpy.html.

9. "Maya Angelou: In disaster, humanity shines" May 27, 2011, CNN, http://www.cnn.com/2011/OPINION/05/25/angelou.interview.joplin/index.html.

10. Related in a lecture presented at Epworth United Methodist Church, Berkeley, California, by Sharon Jacob, associate professor of New Testament, Pacific School of Religion, Berkeley, California, on decolonizing the Bible through the lens of race and gender, August 2020.

PART 4

TOOLS FOR BUILDING BRIDGES

Dr. Lucia Ann McSpadden

CHAPTER 16

Having a Common Language and Understanding

As we continue building intercultural bridges, we need to have a common understanding of what we are communicating. Words convey different meanings to different people in different cultures. Words can be powerful. Let me give you an example.

A Laotian refugee, newly arrived in the US, wanted to look up a retired American missionary, now living in California, who had ministered in the refugee camps in Thailand. The Laotian man revered the missionary, through whose ministry he had become a Christian, so knowing the missionary's home church, he went there to find him. He attended the Sunday worship service; however, when he didn't see the missionary, he asked the pastor where he might find him. The pastor sadly looked at the Laotian man and said, "So sorry, but he kicked the bucket."

The Laotian man was very confused. Why would this missionary kick a bucket, and why was this pastor so sad?

English is not an easy language to learn. Add American clichés, and then we can understand how miscommunication and misunderstanding occurs. In addition, English is not a stagnant language but an evolving one, especially around issues of race, ethnicity, and culture. So, let us try to clarify some concepts and share our understanding of the meaning of some words.

Among the confusing aspects of the expanding understanding of concepts of race, ethnicity, and culture are terms we use to describe each other and our respective cultures. What do we call a person who is an American of Chinese descent? Or an American who immigrated recently from Ghana? Or someone who is a child of a bi-racial marriage?

When did we move from the term "Oriental" to the term "Asian"? From colored to Negro to African American to black American? From Caucasian to European American to white American? From Indian to Native American or indigenous? What are the differences among Chicano, Hispanic, Latino, Latina, and Latinx?

What we call ourselves and others is part history, part governmental determination, and part the identity people want to call themselves. These evolving terms are not stagnant. Turn to the glossary at the end of the book to see the contexts that shape and have shaped the names by which various cultural groups are called. See also chapter 16, "What Do These Words Mean?" and "Race Is a Social Construct," online.

CHAPTER 17

Engaging Across Differences with Respect

As we have been exploring the gospel challenge of engaging with others who have different understandings, different worldviews, and different icebergs, you may have pushed back a bit with the question, "That is all well and good, but how do I do that? I don't think it is so easy or natural." In our current highly polarized and politicized public discourse, yours is a reasonable question.

However, "hope for the church is dependent upon the quality of our conversations. Conversations build relationships, and relationships build hope. Jesus said, 'Where two or three are gathered in my name, I am there among them'" (Matthew 18:20).[1]

Cultural Humility Is Key

You are the learner. The other person is the expert.

A critical foundation for us is that we are trying to understand, wanting to build connections, and hoping to develop good relationships. We are not trying to convince someone to believe the way we believe or act the way we think someone ought to behave. In fact, we are learners listening to and discussing with the experts. This is the foundation of cultural humility, which is the basis of cultural competency. Our desire is to learn so we can behave in a way that will produce positive, connecting relationships. A basic step is to listen, listen, listen. Of course, we listen to others all the time, but how are we listening?

Participating in an international exchange program as a single young adult, I lived with a warm, welcoming family in León, Guanajuato, Mexico. One of the pluses for me was that I had three Mexican "sisters," young single women living at home who were close to my age. My sisters and I did a lot together, which was delightful, along with the added benefit that I markedly improved my Spanish.

Ten years later, I returned to visit them with my husband and three children. Again, I received such a warm welcome; my Mexican "mother" even praised my improved Spanish. Martha was the only one of the sisters still living at home. She was unmarried; her two sisters were both married with children. As Martha and I talked by ourselves, I learned that although she was single, she had fallen in love with a Spanish man while frequently traveling in Spain. They wanted to get married; however, Martha would need to move to Spain, as he was well employed there. When I asked whether she was planning to move, she replied, rather wistfully, that she couldn't do that. I didn't understand; she clearly loved him. She said she knew she had to stay in León with her family; that was her responsibility since her siblings all had other families now. My individualistic self ached for her; in my mind she had sacrificed, turning her back on her own happiness. Perhaps, however, her relationship with and responsibility to her parents superseded her personal desires. I had to listen to her carefully to understand.

The Sacred Art of Listening

In *The Sacred Art of Listening*, Kay Lindahl writes, "Dialogue comes from the Greek *dia*, which means 'through,' combined with *logos*. Dialogue literally means 'words flowing through.' In a flow of conversation, new understandings emerge that might not have been present otherwise. Dialogue, conducted in a spirit of inquiry and a genuine desire to understand, is an open-ended exploration."[2]

In order to develop a more accurate and sensitive interpretation of another person's behavior across cultures and racial identities, one needs to develop relations built upon trust and openness. This involves thoughts, feelings, ideas, and experiences shared back and forth, honoring each other's insights and concerns, and inviting one into relationship with another. When these things are shared, a web of connection is built, perhaps slowly, step by step. (This is in contrast to a monologue, a one-directional exposition.) To accomplish dialogue requires that persons listen intentionally, to learn and understand, not to convince the other. It also requires that we believe what the other person says. Unfortunately, more often than not a person will disagree with what another person reports, saying something like, "That couldn't be true. I think you are being overly sensitive or overreacting."[3]

When I was leading a focus group of laypersons in a church while doing research on cross-cultural clergy assignment, I learned that someone of a different culture had not been believed by members of the majority culture in the church when she complained of being mistreated in a public place. The church's pastor was Hmong, a former refugee from Laos, and now an ordained Methodist minister. The church was located in a rural area with limited grocery stores. The pastor had told me that he and his wife had driven forty-five minutes to shop at another grocery store because she had experienced that the people in their local store were rude and disrespectful to her. The pastor had reported this to the lay leaders, who in turn mentioned it to me. Their response was to make it clear to the pastor that his wife was mistaken because the local storekeepers were well-known and nice persons, so they could not believe that her experience was true. After all, this was not their experience. It should be noted that the wife's English was limited and heavily accented.

The challenge is to believe another person's experience even though it is not what we experience. Our reality may not be the lived reality of another person, particularly a person of color.

Another significant challenge in listening is recognizing that how we communicate is culturally shaped. Social aspects such as gender, age, and social status are more significant in one cultural group than in another. In fact, all of these characteristics are part of social power, which is sometimes overt and sometimes subtle.[4]

You may be aware, for example, that various Asian languages are tonal; the sounds when speaking a word may go higher or lower at different levels. This seems so challenging to me as a native English speaker that I have never tried to learn Chinese. How socially important these tones are was recounted to me by a colleague, a Vietnamese American professor, who recalled having to learn eight different tones as a child. She said it was essential because the particular tone she needed to use indicated the social status of the person to whom she was speaking in relation to her own social status. To make a mistake was to be very disrespectful. She had to be able to do this instantaneously!

Before understanding this, I was set back and irritated when any person from such a cultural context asked my age. You don't ask women in the US how old they are (an iceberg is floating up). Now, I am aware that it is likely that a person may need to know my age in order to address me respectfully. Within the other person's worldview, knowing my relative social status is essential for developing a good relationship with me.

Questions to Ponder . . .

In today's polarized social and political context, it is easy to dismiss the "other." It is tempting to take the stance that there is no use in trying to talk with someone who seems to be coming from another world. The willingness to bridge this puzzling gap in understanding is absent. We are being called to engage with an openness to understand when perhaps we don't want to understand. We are being called to understand; we are not being called to agree. Truly this is a spiritual challenge.

1. How might you listen with respect to someone with whom you disagree?
2. How might you prepare yourself to do so?

See chapter 17, "Active Listening," "Listening Is a Gift," and "Practicing Listening," online.

One of the keys to learning the sacred art of listening is making a commitment to practice every day. How can you incorporate a daily practice into your life?[5]

NOTES

1. John L. Hopkins, "The Power of Conversation," *Circuit Rider* 29, no. 2 (March–April 2005), 8–9.

2. Kay Lindahl, *The Sacred Art of Listening: Forty Reflections for Cultivating the Spiritual Art of Listening* (Woodstock, VT: SkyLight Paths Publishing Company, 2002), 29–30. The title of her book captures the essence of listening as a spiritual practice.

3. More on this in part 4, chapter 18.

4. For further discussion refer to Lucia Ann McSpadden, *Meeting God at the Boundaries: A Manual for Church Leaders* (Nashville: General Board of Higher Education, The United Methodist Church, 2006), 33–36.

5. Lindahl, 32.

CHAPTER 18

Blocking Respectful Communication

Sometimes, when we think we are listening actively and want to be respectful in doing so, we are caught unawares when we hear something that is far removed from our own experience. In earlier chapters we have presented a number of examples; however, we haven't explored our possible responses.

Perhaps you have had the experience of talking to someone about a significant experience in your life when he or she responds in one of the following ways:[1]

"You think that is bad, let me tell you about . . ."

"I know someone who . . ."

"Yeah, but . . ." or "Oh, but . . ."

"Can't you just . . ."

"I don't see or feel that!"

"It seems clear to me that . . ."

How would you describe your feelings when this is the response you receive? Are you eager to continue sharing from your life? Do you change the subject? Do you get into a disagreement?

Overall, your experience or feelings are being denied. Although you are not being called a liar or a fool, clearly the other person knows how you should have handled the experience, how you should feel, or diminishes the importance of your experience. Whatever the specific comments, you're not likely to be eager to explore more deeply.

Perhaps one of the more surprising stories about Jesus is found in Mark 7:24-30, entitled "The Syrophoenician Woman's Faith." In reading this passage, you may have been as surprised at Jesus' behavior as I was.

Questions to Ponder . . .

Take a moment to reread the passage and reflect upon the interaction between Jesus and the Syrophoenician woman. If possible, do this in a small group or in pairs.

The cultural and religious understandings at that time add depth to this recounting. Women did not speak to unrelated men in public. Jews despised Gentiles and avoided contact with them. They looked down upon them because they understood Gentiles to be as "impure" as dogs.

1. What seem to be the world views or assumptions shaping Jesus' behavior?
2. How would you describe Jesus' response? What verbs and/or adjectives would you use?
3. What changed in the interaction between Jesus and the woman?
4. What seemed to cause Jesus to change his response to one of compassion?
5. How do ways of listening enter into the drama of this story?
6. What have you learned from this uncomfortable story?

Do Not Use "Why" Questions

One of the most powerful relationship blockers is the communication response, "Why?" "Why" causes persons to feel that they have to defend themselves. Think about how you feel when someone asks you, "Why did you do that?" I immediately feel as if I am being challenged and that the other person thinks something is wrong with what I have said or done. I sense we are moving into an argument. I want to draw back; I don't want to engage, or I want to fight back, depending upon various social factors. None of these responses will engender an interest or a willingness to extend myself further. The chance of developing a meaningful relationship becomes much less likely; I will be more careful around this person. Of course, there are non-personal why questions that don't cause such a negative reaction ("Why are the stores closing so early?") or caring questions ("Why is your arm in a sling; is it hurting?").

Yes–But/Yes–And

When people gather together to plan some action, presenting and engaging with everyone's ideas and skills is important. Often, the planning will require several meetings. For purposes of our thinking, let's assume a group wants to celebrate an achievement by the church youth group. The idea is to have a party. The plan needs to be put into action in a short time. How might our discussion style be a communication blocker or a door opener to creativity? For example, how might the discussion be hindered when the response is a consistent "yes, but"? How might the discussion be encouraged and even become more creative when the response is a "yes, and"? See the online exercise "Yes/But, Yes/And" for chapter 18.

Self-Awareness Is a Major Key

Self-awareness, as we have stressed, is a key, perhaps the major key, to developing cultural humility and cultural competence. This is especially important when we are engaging in the context of social inequalities; feelings are often raw, and persons can be apprehensive about discrimination, prejudice, or disrespect.

A personally awkward, unsurprising family situation happened when my son and I were talking about a work challenge that he was facing. I offered my recommendation of what he should do rather than listening to his feelings. He immediately responded with, "I am an adult; I can manage my own life; don't tell me what to do!" Any meaningful conversation stopped. My intent was to be supportive. The impact of my suggestion was to challenge his competence.

A much more intense personal experience occurred in my church when several of us women, including my "white self" and several African American women, were planning a series of adult forums focused on social justice. We had never done one about transgendered persons, and I was promoting a series with that focus. The African American women were insistent about the time not being right for this focus given what was happening regarding racial issues. They thought that we should prioritize racial injustices. I felt we had already done quite a bit of that and so continued to press for a transgender series. These women were long-time friends, and though the impact for them was a dismissing of the deep and continuing pain and danger black persons experience daily, they hung in with me. One stayed with me for over an hour answering my questions and countering my analysis with her insights. It took me a long time to understand more clearly how my intent of broadening our program impacted them given the reality of their lives. In the process, they asserted that they did understand the discrimination transgender persons face but experienced the impact of my pushing as not listening, not hearing their pain. I am so grateful to them for their patience with me!

Wise caution suggests that we should reflect on the possible impact of our words and comments, for when our intent clearly has delivered an unintentional negative impact, a learning opportunity presents itself to those who are willing to grab hold of it. If possible, you may be able to find out how your response was perceived; if so, you have information to reflect upon and guide you for the future. (See also chapter 18, "Relationship Building and Effective Communication" and "Culture as an Iceberg," online.)

Another way for us to strengthen self-awareness is to reflect on our reactions when we hear something that we can't believe to be true. What might be our fallback position that leads us to deny the possibility of what we have heard from another person? We will explore this further in part 5.

NOTES

1. These responses are adapted and expanded from "Notice Communication Blockers," developed by Dr. Jamie Washington and adapted by Partnership Consulting, Inc., 2020.

CHAPTER 19

Perceptions and Assumptions

Perception is the process of selecting, organizing, and interpreting the world. We do this all of the time in different ways, for better or worse.[1]

Selective attention occurs when we notice some things and not others. What we pay attention to is based on our background and cultural experiences.

Selective exposure happens when we expose ourselves to familiar and comfortable things and avoid uncomfortable or unfamiliar ones.

Selective recall is what we do when we remember some things and forget others.

First impressions tend to have a strong influence on us, so being cautious about them is wise because they can lead us to wrong understandings. A good thing to do is to reflect on the difference between goals and the behavior that is expected in order to reach them. We can assume, for example, that all persons want to be respected and want to show respect. How to demonstrate respect can vary significantly. In one culture a sign of respect is to look directly at someone's eyes. In another culture, a sign of respect is to look down and never to look someone in the eye. Yet in both instances, respect is intended. So many nonverbal behaviors are used to show respect. If cultural values shift, the meaning of a specific behavior can also shift; for example, should a man hold the door open for a woman? We cannot observe people's values or goals; we can only observe their behavior.

"If I assume that because someone behaves differently from me, he or she has different goals and values, I could (easily) be wrong. If I assume that because the person behaves similarly, we share the same goals and values, I could also be wrong. *This is a critical distinction in developing cultural competency.*"[2]

Any behavior experienced in an intercultural or interracial context can be interpreted in two ways: by the meaning given to it by the person who does the action, and by the meaning given to it by the person who observes or experiences the action.[3]

Reflecting on the many stories we have presented points to the fact that bewilderment is a common experience that can lead to misinterpreting the meaning and intent of what we are experiencing. How easy it is for us to jump to conclusions, and often incorrect ones. Instead of drawing wrong conclusions, how might we thoughtfully respond when bewildered by another's behavior? How might we avoid using our cultural framework to assess meaning and value? In order to use effectively whatever tools we have, we must hold before us the foundational and essential approach of assuming positive intent.

One approach to assessing meaning and value is set out in the diagram The Process of Adjustment.[4]

In the diagram on page 86 one phrase is highlighted in **bold**. This is done to call attention to the **choice point**, the point to stop, slow down, take a deep breath, and reflect before acting. What choice will you make? Are you going to move forward to learn more before making a judgment? Are you going to withdraw to retreat or to foster a negative reaction? The question here is, What is my goal? If I am focused on being right no matter what, I am not likely to move forward. If my goal is to

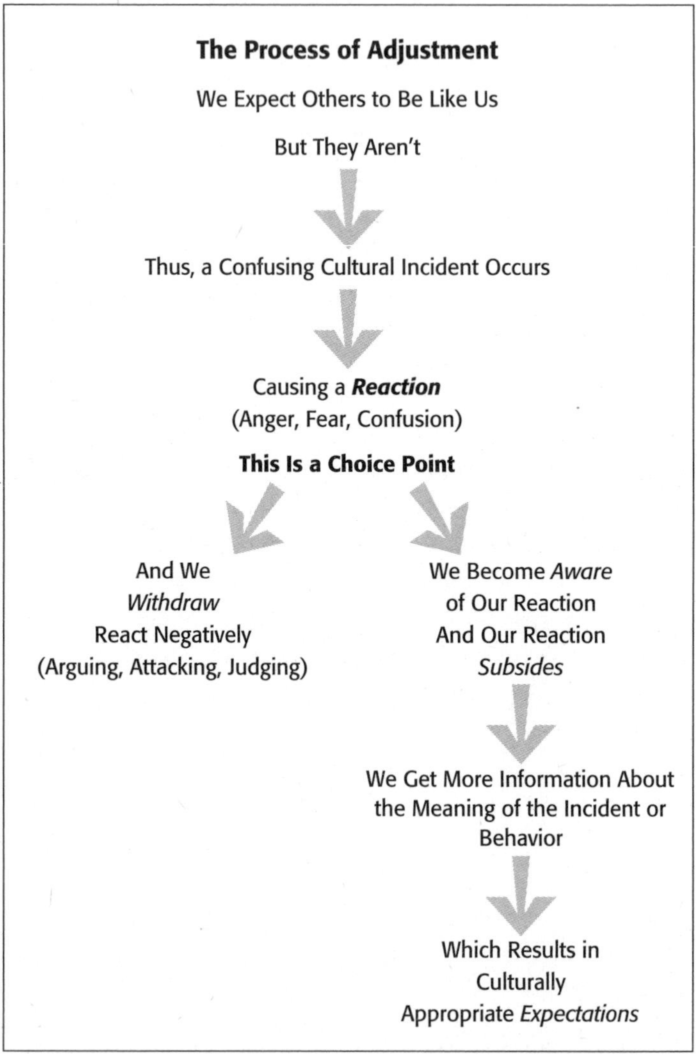

The Process of Adjustment

We Expect Others to Be Like Us

But They Aren't

↓

Thus, a Confusing Cultural Incident Occurs

↓

Causing a ***Reaction***
(Anger, Fear, Confusion)

This Is a Choice Point

↙ And We
Withdraw
React Negatively
(Arguing, Attacking, Judging)

↘ We Become *Aware*
of Our Reaction
And Our Reaction
Subsides

↓

We Get More Information About the Meaning of the Incident or Behavior

↓

Which Results in Culturally Appropriate *Expectations*

develop a good or trusting relationship, then I will use my emotional and intellectual energy to go forward toward understanding. Cultural competence is grounded in cultural humility, which is to say that we understand ourselves as being learners; we recognize that the other is the knowledgeable one, the teacher. Cultural competence is the ability to shift perspective appropriately and the willingness to adapt behavior in order to be effective in the cultural context.

Gathering Information to Deepen Understanding

Our tendency to misperceive and misunderstand frequently and with automatic responses is understandable. However, we can stop and reflect upon our reactions and try to understand by asking, "What is going on with me?" Assuming a positive intent on the part of the other person, we may be led to try to find out more about his or her intentions. We can ask the other person questions, listen to them, observe them, and develop more than one interpretation of their behavior. When we do this, we usually abandon our initial reaction and develop more culturally appropriate expectations.[5] We may try out new behaviors in order to relate more effectively.

A checklist may help to give some structure to the process of getting the needed information. Going through this list may provide a guide for getting to your learning goal.

Identify the variety of resources you have available.

Do you know people with intercultural experience?

What relationships might you need to build?

What specific behaviors will you likely need to cultivate to get the needed information?

What support do you need to achieve that goal?

What would be your basic, overall goal?

Engaging in this process takes time. We come face to face with the high value placed on time and its management in the US worldview. We save time, waste time, manage time, gain time, lose time, and take time. As you go through your days, become aware of how time is a commodity to be used. It takes intention and concentration to slow down, listen, watch, seek out information, re-engage, practice. Commitment is needed; the rewards are high. Be aware that "the key ingredients of working in another culture are listening, relationships, respect, and time. What is needed is a continuity of relationship in which we extend ourselves deeply."[6]

Gathering the needed information in order to understand the meaning and intent of another person's behavior requires some research. One of the most effective ways to gain an understanding of confusing intercultural happenings is to consult with one or more bridge persons.

Of course, we don't always have a bridge person to reach out to. There are other, less direct ways, to get insight—movies, novels, podcasts, museums, and library research into a specific culture. Another way to gain insight is by visiting a church with members of the culture that interests you. Visiting a church serves several purposes, including the benefit of experiencing worship with Christian brothers and sisters, and providing an opportunity to begin relationships that could lead to finding one or more bridge persons. My experience is that persons are often pleased to guide and teach if they sense that you are sincere about learning. Check out the suggestions above for information-gathering questions. Even frequenting places where people gather—cafes, restaurants, sports games—is a fun way to observe behavior long enough so that it doesn't feel quite as strange. You might even learn to like some new food!

Our tendency to jump to conclusions without reflection and analysis may best be prevented by our using a structured approach. The approach presented in Describe, Investigate, Evaluate (D.I.E., on page 89) helps us do that.[7]

Description is what one sees and/or hears: the "objective facts." Not all observers notice the same things: some might notice the location; others the time; others the gestures a person used. For example, "Mary walked into the room at 7:15. She did not sit down." "The man gave his opinions without being called upon by the chairperson."

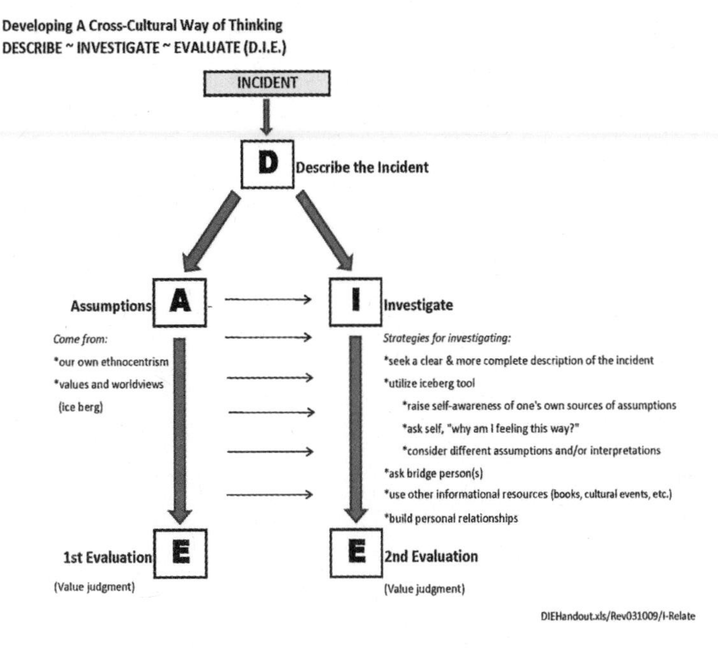

Interpretation has to do with what one thinks about what one sees and/or hears. For example, "Mary does not respect the time of others." "The man thinks his ideas are more important than anyone else's ideas." These are interpretations based on the viewer's own assumptions and values, which typically arise from one's cultural background.

Evaluation has to do with what one feels about what one sees and/or hears. Typically, these evaluations take on a moral or ethical tone: that person is a good person or a bad person; that person is untrustworthy or not trustworthy. The viewer's values are the issue, not the person's actual behavior. Terms such as "right," "wrong," "should," "ought," "weird," or "strange" are usually evaluative or judgmental statements.

With D.I.E. in mind, we have a tool for avoiding misunderstandings and negativism. To use this tool, see chapter 19, "Using D.I.E., Clarify Your Reactions" and "D.I.E. Analysis," in the online workbook.

NOTES

1. Lucia Ann McSpadden, *Meeting God at the Boundaries: A Manual for Church Leaders* (Nashville: General Board of Higher Education, The United Methodist Church, 2006), 30–31.

2. Donna M. Stringer and Patricia A. Cassiday, *52 Activities for Exploring Value Differences* (Yarmouth, ME: Intercultural Press, 2003), xii, emphasis added; quoted in McSpadden, *Meeting God at the Boundaries*, 30–31.

3. Craig Storti and Laurette Bennhold-Samaan, *Culture Matters: The Peace Corps Cross-Cultural Workbook* (Washington, DC: US Government Printing Office, n.d.), 20.

4. Adapted from Craig Storti, *The Art of Crossing Cultures* (Yarmouth, ME: Intercultural Press, 1989), 61–62. Reproduced by permission of Nicholas Brealey Publishing.

5. McSpadden, *Meeting God at the Boundaries*, 31.

6. Greg Mortenson, *Three Cups of Tea: One Man's Mission to Fight Terrorism and Build Nations—One School at a Time* (New York: Viking Press, 2006), heard on NPR, Forum, December 11, 2009.

7. The D.I.E diagram is adapted from the Describe, Interpret, and Evaluate model developed by Janet Bennett, the director of the Summer Institute of Intercultural Communication in Portland, Oregon. Her model is widely used among intercultural communication practitioners and academics. This particular adaptation was developed by the Rev. Dr. Marie Onwubuariri in her work with i-Relate.

CHAPTER 20

Becoming a Cultural Detective

A visual model can be a helpful way to remember a complex social reality. Dianne Hofner Saphiere, the developer of the Cultural Detective approach, offers this model to remind us of the factors we need to engage when analyzing an intercultural interaction.[1] You might notice that action is depicted along with description. We will engage the action in the final step.

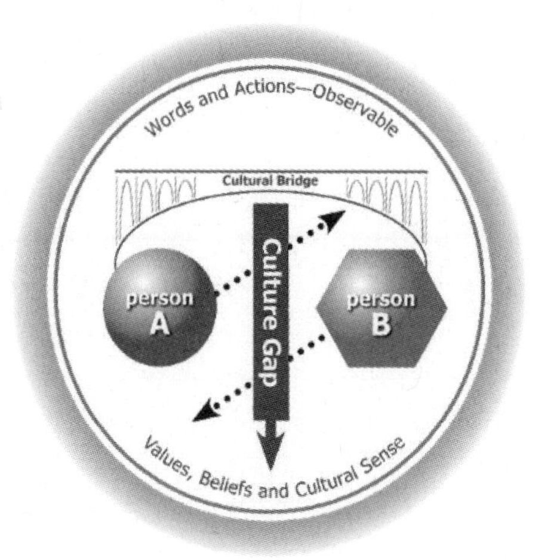

The Basic Steps in Being a Cultural Detective

Describe

The first important action is to *describe as clearly as possible* what happened. You will remember when we discussed the D.I.E. dynamic how necessary it is to be *disciplined* in doing this. What *behavior* did you see? What *words* did the persons involved use? How and when did they speak and to whom? What *facial expressions* did you notice and by whom? Overall, does your description match what a video with sound would show?

You may notice that many words are highlighted in italics. Using italics helps point out the challenge that we face when we try to describe an observation without adding *our meaning* to the description. Taking the leap to interpretation is so natural that it would seem that our cultural values are hard-wired. However, what is essential is that we only *describe literally what we observe* because *we do not know the meaning* given to the other person's *behavior or action*. If we are disciplined to just observe, then giving a literal description is easier to do. When we are *engaged as participants*, observing is more challenging, so discipline is critical.

Positive Intent

Assume positive intent of all involved. Investigate to discover what *values and beliefs* might be underlying the actions described. A first approach could be to sit with the description and brainstorm (either by yourself or with others) the possible values. Of course, brainstorming this way is limited by one's knowledge and experience. If you, yourself, are part of the situation, *self-awareness* is critical. In fact, even if you are an outside observer, being self-aware will help you to be insightful. Again, a bridge person is incredibly helpful. Other ways to investigate are listed previously (see the checklist in chapter 19, on page 87). When you feel reasonably satisfied with what you have determined to be the possible values guiding the behavior or action of the persons involved, the next step will be even more dynamic.

Build a Bridge

The question now becomes what might be *ways to build a bridge* so that *all persons experience that their values and beliefs are being recognized and respected.*

Let's picture a bridge over a body of water. For the bridge to function safely, the pillars on each end need to be firmly grounded. The same is true here. The beliefs and values of the persons are the pillars that will support the bridge to relationships and mutual regard.

However, some compromises will be necessary in order to build strong pillars. For example, in the case study in the D.I.E. discussion online (chapter 19), the Korean pastor would still need to report to the church board, but the white senior pastor could share with him the type of information the board members want, and in what format. Then, the Korean pastor could write his report and submit it prior to the meeting. By his so doing, the board would get what it wanted (although not in the way they are accustomed) and the Korean pastor would remain in control of his position without—according to his thinking—having to defend his work. Were it not for such compromises, there would never be a functioning bridge.

Call on creativity. Open your mind to possible options by engaging more minds to allow more ideas to flow. Think of persons who might work with you on this because when you are involved in the situation and considering alternatives that you can feel good about, having persons to explore with you in a supportive way is helpful.

Build New Pillars

In some situations, you or others may be able to try out building the pillars for the bridge and the solutions you or others think would be effective. If the result is positive, celebrate. If not, go back to the basics with new information. (See chapter 20, "Cultural Detective Approach Analysis," and the case study, "To Sing or Not to Sing," online.)

NOTES

1. This image, developed by Dianne Hofner Saphiere, is used with all the Culture Detective educational materials. Used here by permission.

CHAPTER 21

Differences in Communication Styles

Many people are familiar with recognizing the differences between an extrovert's and an introvert's style of engaging in a conversation. Since the mainstream US culture rewards extroverted behavior, we sometimes pass over an introvert who is quiet in a group or who wants to think things over before responding. As an extrovert married to a strong introvert, I had to be educated on how to communicate effectively with my husband. Often, he would say, "Could you just get to the point?" because an abundance of detail meant he needed time to reflect. I would respond, "I am getting there; this all relates to what happened." I learned that I would need to modify my communication style if I wanted to connect with him.

In a similar fashion, cultures have their own culturally shaped, unique communication styles. Since people tend to think that their communication style is natural, confusion abounds. Remember that when something seems natural, it is cultural! Challenges occur when one is faced with communicating in different cultural styles. The following discussion is linked to using the D.I.E. process effectively. Remember, too, *interpretation* has to do with what one thinks about what one sees and/or hears. *Evaluation* has to do with what one feels about what one sees and/or hears.

Intercultural Communication Styles

Although there are numerous differences in communication styles from culture to culture, likely the most important for us in the US are the indirect/direct or high context/low context contrasts.[1]

Indirect Communication Style

Indirect communication style is characteristic of homogeneous and relational social contexts, often referred to as high context cultures. In such cultures, personal relationships and the status linked to those relationships structure society at all levels. People know and understand each other quite well. Because they have a shared context, history, and knowledge, they have less need to be explicit; therefore, they rely less on words to convey meaning, especially the literal meaning of the word. Since these societies tend to be relational rather than individualistic, people work closely together and each one knows what everyone else knows. People often convey meaning by manipulating the context, for example, being sure the appropriate person is present for a discussion. "The overriding goal of communication exchange is maintaining harmony and saving face."[2] Focus is on the people involved since they all are part of a larger group, the community. The list below may give you a feel for the techniques of indirect communication.

Using a qualified yes to mean no

Telling a story as a way to say no delicately

Changing the subject to avoid saying no

Asking a question to give a negative answer

Returning to the previous discussion to signal disagreement

A Filipina colleague guiding my understanding said it is important never to ask a yes or no question to persons who function indirectly because it puts them in a very uncomfortable situation. Her recommendation is to approach a request with a choice, for example, "The committee needs to meet to plan the event. Will Monday evening or Thursday morning be better for you?" This approach provides an avenue for them to respond with their preference or to offer another time.

Direct Communication Style

Direct communication style is characteristic of cultures like the United States that tend to be heterogeneous and individualistic. Often, these cultures are called low context cultures because persons cannot use the context of personal relationships to engage meaningfully with others. Less can be assumed or known about the other person in a culture where people prefer independence, self-reliance, and a greater emotional distance from each other. They have less shared history and knowledge, so they cannot rely on not doing or not saying something in order to communicate. They can't depend on nonverbal behavior, and they don't look for meaning behind the words. Instead, in low-context cultures, people rely not only on words but also on words being interpreted literally. Communication is explicit and focuses on the issue being discussed. Being direct is not interpreted as aggressive or personal but as "just the facts, ma'am, just the facts." There is a caveat in that many Americans do not prefer the direct style of speech; however, direct style is the expected speech style formed by northern European immigrants—the socially dominant group today—during the founding of the US. (See chapter 21, "Direct and Indirect Speech," "Decoding Indirectness," and "A Self-Assessment," online.)

Linear and Circular Communication Styles

The linear style of communication is embedded in direct communication style (as we have discussed above) and is familiar to those who have lived in the US for an extended period of time, whether or not we use it as our preferred style.

Circular communication style is often used by persons from Latin America and, depending upon specific cultures, by some indirect speakers. I encountered this, to my frustration, as I read manuscripts from colleagues in Nicaragua and Bolivia. I would read and read, trying to get to the point of the discussion. I was exhausted by the end because I was automatically looking for a straight, linear style.

When directly talking with someone who uses a circular style to communicate, it is easy to assume that the person is vague, unfocused, and perhaps not too clear thinking. One might even assume that the person is trying to hide an issue by giving so much detail. A Japanese student of mine, who naturally used a similar style but had learned the direct style needed in her classes, explained to me that using a direct style is an insult to the listener. The direct style assumes that the listener is not smart enough or clever enough to understand the basic ideas. That caused me to think about my expectations again.

NOTES

1. Edward T. Hall, *The Silent Language* (New York: Doubleday, 1959), introduced the terms "low context" and "high context" cultures. He is often called the father of anthropology. A number of videos on YouTube present the difference between indirect and direct communication. What Is the Difference Between a High-Context and Low-Context Culture? Search for in YouTube for video options to view.

2. Craig Storti and Laurette Bennhold-Samaan, *Culture Matters: The Peace Corps Cross-Cultural Workbook* (Washington, DC: U.S. Government Printing Office, n.d.), 78.

CHAPTER 22

Emotional and Nonverbal Communication

In addition to the communication styles we've already discussed, there are two other kinds of communication: an emotional style and nonverbal communication.

Emotional Style of Communication

The emotional style of communication has come to the forefront as our nation confronts, yet again, the racial realities and the inequities undergirded by deep-seated prejudices. Emotional styles may, at first glance, seem far removed from these fraught social dynamics; however, accepted modes of public debate differ markedly. For example, a conflict often exists between what blacks versus whites believe to be acceptable emotional levels of speech and styles of communication. Such stylistic conflict reveals the potent effect of racial and social differences. The misunderstandings that result reinforce underlying beliefs and assign value connected to race. All of this dynamic is embedded and shaped by the social power struggle between white norms and black norms.[1]

In the US mainstream (white) social context, the dominant (white) culture is socially, reflexively, and without thought understood as normative—the way everyone should behave. Therefore, it is not surprising that alternative ways of communicating are negatively assessed. The cultural norms guiding how people should speak to each other are frequently not focused upon when persons from black and white cultures are interacting but ignoring cultural norms in this context can be and usually is destructive to relationships, and it strengthens prejudices.

Speaking generally, black culture allows for more emotional expression than white culture. Qualities of individual self-assertion, such as self-expression, forthrightness, and emotional expressiveness are highly valued within black style. The communication style is high-keyed, animated, interpersonal, and confrontational, but not antagonistic. Argument is used to persuade, not to attack.

If a black person is engaging in lively debate and gets "emotional," it means he or she is connected to the discussion. He or she is not about to "lose it" or become violent as a white person might if behaving in the same manner (according to white cultural norms). Often, blacks are advocating for a truth that is significant to them. They are showing that they care deeply about an issue.

By contrast, white communication style's goal is "neutral objectivity with regard to the truth that is 'out there,' a truth that is to be discovered."[2] To be more specific, I am referring to middle-class, mainstream whites. This is the group that is indicated when speaking of the norms of the socially dominant group. The communication mode for this powerful group is relatively low-keyed, dispassionate, impersonal, and non-challenging. Argument functions to ventilate anger and hostility. It doesn't function as a process of persuasion. Culturally, whites relate to their topic as spokespersons, not advocates. How deeply a person cares about or believes in the idea is considered irrelevant to its fundamental value. Whites hope to avoid dynamic confrontation, which they equate with conflict.

"Whites invariably interpret black anger and aggressiveness (in speech) as more provocative and threatening than do blacks."[3] A white person might say, "Will you just calm down!" Blacks accuse whites of being insincere, of not caring, perhaps hiding what they truly believe or an agenda they intend to carry forward. One African American man, quoted in Kochman's work, stated, "You don't need to worry; I am still talking. When I *stop* talking, then you might need to worry."[4]

Monitoring their speech when discussing issues with a white person is yet another stress in the daily life of many black persons who don't want their concerns to be dismissed. An African American professor and church friend reflected while speaking to me that she often had to intervene at the school on behalf of her daughter with a special learning need. She thought carefully about how she would present her concerns. She said that it was important not to be perceived as "an angry black woman" so that the teachers would listen to her and work with her to support her daughter.

Another significant difference in communication style between white and black persons is whether or not an assertion about behavior, social benefit or the lack thereof, and social status is understood. For example, blacks making a general accusation of "white privilege" are referring to how the social system functions to provide unequal benefits to various racial or ethnic groups. They are not asserting all whites are privileged. Typically, when a white person hears an accusation of "white privilege," he or she assumes it is a personal indictment or description. We have experienced this consistently when facilitating intercultural workshops with white people. "What are you saying! You don't know me; you have no idea about my life. I was raised by a single mother on welfare."

Nonverbal Communication

We have been discussing verbal communication, but there is another powerful style of communication: nonverbal communication. A substantial portion of our communication is nonverbal. In fact, most experts agree that 70 to 93 percent of all communication is nonverbal.[5] Every day we respond to and enact nonverbal cues, including facial expressions, loudness or tone of voice, eye gaze, gestures, personal distance, touching, and posture. These signals are often so subtle that we are not consciously aware of them in ourselves or others; also, they are often automatic. However subtle, they are a major component in our communication. They impact how people interpret meaning in conversations. In group situations, it is helpful to pay attention to one another's body language as well. This is especially important if you consider the power of the group and its propensity for high context/indirect speakers. (See chapter 22, "Interpret Nonverbal Behaviors" and "Showing Emotions," in the online workbook.)

Gestures, which are among the most direct and obvious body language signals, vary widely between cultures and can be a source of significant misunderstandings. In one culture, a handshake is a friendly greeting gesture while in another culture it shows an ignorance of status. In yet another, especially if it is a very hard handshake, it conveys power over the other person. A common gesture in the United States means "okay," but in Europe, the same gesture can connote that you are nothing. In parts of Latin America, it can be a vulgar expression. Because we cannot know all the subtleties of different cultural gestures, jumping to conclusions is not wise.

With regard to social space, how much distance between persons is comfortable and seems "right" varies by culture. Edward Hall, an anthropologist, is known for his study of how social space is utilized to experience feeling comfortable. He described four different types of social spaces: intimate (0-18 inches), personal (18 inches to 4 feet), social (4 feet to 10 feet), and public (over 10 feet.) When he took into account cultural variances, he identified two basic categories of social distance: contact and non-contact. In contact cultures (e.g., Italian, Arab, French, Latin American, Mexican), physical touching between acquaintances is encouraged and necessary for good personal relationships. For non-contact cultures (e.g., US, Sweden, Japan, and most Southeast Asian communities), touching is reserved for only the most intimate acquaintances.[6]

We have demonstrated social distancing in our workshops to hilarious effect. People are paired up and asked to carry on a conversation on a non-controversial topic. One person is instructed to keep a distance of at least four to six feet from the other. The second person is instructed to keep very close to the person while speaking, touching him or her. Can you imagine the scene? If you had a video, you would see the couples moving all around the room. One person is backing up as the other person comes in close. Finally, everyone is either laughing or becoming very frustrated. If you put this into different cultural frames, it would be like an Italian speaking with a Japanese. Personally, I am very much a hugger and a toucher, so I had to totally alter my spatial behavior when I lived in Japan. When I lived in Mexico, oh, how comfortable that was! This is an example of what is meant when we say to be culturally competent one needs to adapt one's behavior in order to function effectively in another culture. Sometimes that is comfortable; sometimes it is not so comfortable, at least at the beginning.

As we reflect upon nonverbal behavior, be aware that this is an area where implicit biases come strongly into play. You may feel very uncomfortable with another person without realizing why. Be self-aware, asking yourself why you have this feeling. Be as specific as you can. If you are in a setting where there are others of the same ethnic or racial identity as the person with whom you are speaking, look around and watch behavior.

Key Points in Communicating Interculturally

Seek first to understand.

Assume positive intent.

Don't take it personally.

As we continue to explore other tools for developing cultural humility and cultural competency, keep these key points in mind. They are the bedrock for using the tools effectively so you can reach the goal of establishing trusting relationships.

NOTES

1. For extensive exploration of black and white communication styles, see Thomas Kochman, *Black and White Styles in Conflict* (Chicago: University of Chicago Press, 1983).
2. Kochman, *Black and White Styles in Conflict*, 21.
3. Kochman, *Black and White Styles in Conflict*, 44.
4. Kochman, *Black and White Styles in Conflict*, 43.
5. "Nonverbal Communication: How Body Language & Nonverbal Cues Are Key," February 18, 2020, Lifesize.com, https://www.lifesize.com/en/blog/speaking-without-words/.
6. Edward Hall, *The Silent Language* (New York: Doubleday, 1959), introduced and expanded the analysis of social space.

CHAPTER 23

Tools for Dealing with Conflict

Cultural groups have developed over time expected or approved ways of dealing with conflict. We have discussed that earlier regarding emotional levels of engagement. Now, we want to focus specifically on dealing with conflict interculturally. (See chapter 23, "How Different Cultures Deal with Conflict," online.)

Cross-Cultural Styles of Conflict Resolution

Denial or Suppression

The person tries to solve the problem by denying its existence. Differences are played down and surface harmony is preserved.

Advantage: If the issue is relatively unimportant, this style allows a cooling-off period or lets time heal the problem.

Disadvantage: If the issue is important, this style allows the problem to build into a more severe situation that is difficult to solve.

Power or Authority[2]

A formal authority, position, majority rule, or persuasive authority settles the conflict. Power is used to impose a solution.

Advantage: When speed or efficiency is most important, this style may be effective. It also demonstrates the status of the person or group in authority. (Authority is often used in hierarchical societies.)

Disadvantage: The people who lose the conflict may feel devalued and/or may even cause disruptions in the future to get even. In a low-context society this approach can cause a strong negative reaction and increased hostility and/or conflict.

Third-Party Intermediary

Two people who are having a conflict use a third person as a go-between to convey messages to each other. Direct mention of the problem to the involved people is avoided, but the go-between is aware of everyone's position. (See the online case study, also referenced in chapter 20, "To Sing or Not to Sing.")

Advantage: This style allows the preservation of surface harmony while still addressing the conflict and possibly resolving it.

Disadvantage: The conflict may become confused and more complicated because of misinterpretations by the third-party intermediary. Persons involved in the conflict may not think their feelings have been sufficiently understood.

Group Consensus

A group is used to share ideas about resolving a conflict and coming to a decision on action that is agreed to by the whole group.

Advantage: A group may come up with better ideas for resolving the conflict than could an individual alone. The whole group's agreement to a resolution is a powerful, non-authoritarian influence on the people in the conflict.

Disadvantage: The style is time-consuming and requires a commitment to hang in there. This style requires a high level of already established trust. The group may avoid facing difficult issues and concentrate on a relatively unimportant aspect of the conflict. (People can feel very exposed.)

Note: Often, participants have an unspoken expectation of group process skills. The level of such skills can and likely will determine whether or not this approach succeeds in having all participants experience that their insights and concerns have been fully addressed.

Direct Discussion

Individuals are involved in an open conflict talk with one another about their perceptions of and feelings about the problem and possible solutions. (This approach is commonly valued in low context/direct communication societies.)

Advantage: The conflict is clear and understood by the involved people. Resolving the conflict is supported by the participants since they came up with a solution.

Disadvantage: Involved individuals might not have the desire or the skills to engage in constructive confrontation, causing them to feel worse afterward. Time and commitment to this process may be lacking. Power differences can make this a one-sided process.

Often gender becomes significant; direct confrontation is more likely to be a fallback approach for men. Historically, women have been socialized to avoid initiating direct confrontation. Recently for younger women, there may be more willingness and skill to engage conflict directly, but the iceberg socialization for women remains.

Patience and Waiting It Out[3]

Individuals are clear about the conflict and about their own goals. However, they do not openly and strongly push for their position. They stay in relationship with the other party or parties and continue to work on the issue. This has been called the "water wearing away the sandstone" approach.

Advantage: People are not pushed into more extreme positions. If the relationships are well developed, people's positions will change and the situation will be resolved. People experience being respected.

Disadvantage: This takes a significant commitment of time and an honest concern to develop the relationships needed. The goal may not in any regard be reached.

For all of us, the challenge occurs when our preferred style differs from others, and we must choose an approach that will allow all the parties to be equally engaged. Clearly, compromise and adaptation will be necessary. Since we can control only our behavior, we are the ones who must discern and act upon a possible modified avenue to constructive engagement. The word *constructive* is used intentionally. Conflict, if managed effectively, brings to our awareness important issues that need to be addressed. Many of us would prefer to avoid or ignore conflict because it can be painful and/or even fearful. This is especially true if we are afraid of losing friends or influence; however, when we avoid or ignore conflict, negative experiences and feelings fester. The necessary beginning for us is to recognize as much as possible the different styles of engagement that are operating. The distinctions listed above under the heading "Cross-Cultural Styles of Conflict Resolution" above can be a helpful guide, especially if we remember that there are variations within a cultural group. Not all people who have been socialized in a culture to do group consensus, for example, are comfortable or skilled in that approach. There are individual preferences or skills. However, the description lays out the basic variations. Review your understanding of high context/indirect communication patterns in comparison with low context/direct communication patterns. These differences are frequently present.

Questions to Ponder . . .

1. Referring to the descriptions outlining different cultural approaches to managing conflict, decide whether a given approach illustrates a high context/indirect or a low context/direct communication. If you are not sure, write down the reasons why you are not sure.
2. Again, using these descriptions, identify your preferred style. List the ways that you learned this style. Think of persons, family life, school experiences, social gatherings, work life, and so forth.
3. Reflect on conflict situations (minor or major) in which you have participated. In what ways did you participate? How did you engage? In what ways were you satisfied with your participation? In what ways were you dissatisfied? As best as you can remember, how would you describe the styles that were utilized?

See chapter 23, the workbook exercise "How Different Cultures Deal with Conflict," the case studies in "Identify Conflict Styles and Who Uses Them," and the exercises "Bodily Reactions to Negativity in Conflict Situations" and "How to Develop Trusting Cross-Cultural/Racial Relationships," online.

NOTES

1. Adapted from Milton J. Bennett, "Critical Incidents in an Intercultural Conflict-Resolution Exercise," in S. M. Fowler and M. G. Mumford, eds., *Intercultural Sourcebook: Cross-Cultural Training Methods* (Yarmouth, ME: Intercultural Press, 1995), 147–56.

2. Power is also an issue in any of the other styles. When there is unequal power between people in conflict, any of these styles can be used to impose a solution that favors those in power. Therefore, the specific power dynamics must be taken into consideration.

3. This point was contributed by the Rev. Kathryn Choy-Wong.

PART 5

LEARNING TO UNLEARN

Rev. Dr. Dale M. Weatherspoon

CHAPTER 24

Institutional Racism

Seemingly sensitive to the marginalization of racial/ethnic groups within their area, the California/Nevada region of the United Methodist church called a "hearing" meeting. The goal was for denomination staff to hear from ethnic minority church leaders about their experiences in order to lay a foundation for progress toward effective inclusion. I was delighted to be invited, especially since I was a member of our Conference Commission on Religion and Race.

What a disaster! The ethnic minority leaders were there prepared to share. Everyone was welcomed, and the intention of the meeting was again presented. I was a "fly on the wall." However, the meeting became a forum for the denomination staff to talk to the folks rather than to listen to them. Initially, I thought that approach was just laying out the context of the denominational system at that time. As this top-down presentation went on and on, it became clear that there was no interest in either listening to or learning from the ethnic minority clergy. Such disrespect, such power over rather than collaboration with was appalling! To this day, some of us continue to reflect on how that experience decreased trust in the church as an institution. —Shan

While pastoring a suburban white church with a number of Filipinos, I noticed most of the Filipinos were not serving on committees or in leadership roles. I asked members of the nominating committee why this was so. They stated that the Filipinos said no when asked.

I spoke with a few of the Filipino members, and they informed me that they were asked only once. I inquired as to what this meant. I learned that it was their custom to be asked three times. The first time their response would be one of humility and surprise that they were being asked. The second time they knew the sincerity of the invitation. This led them into a time of prayer, discerning God's will for them. The third time they would give their answer.

When I relayed this to the nominating committee, their response was, "We have a list of members to ask. We call and ask and move down our lists until the slots are filled. We have to complete our work by a certain date. We don't have time to ask three times and wait." I shared that if we wanted to be an inclusive church, this approach was unacceptable, and we would have to find another way. I suggested that we begin the nominating process earlier to provide our Filipino members with the time they needed for discernment. The committee reluctantly agreed. The result was that our Filipino members began saying yes to committee assignments and began serving.

Once our Filipino members began attending the committee meetings, our committees became more diverse. Yet, after two or three meetings, they had stopped attending. When I noticed their absence, I asked a few members why they stopped attending. The response was a learning moment in communication styles and differences.

The ones I spoke to said, "We come, we sit and listen, but nobody asks us what we think. They don't invite us to share our thoughts, ideas, or opinions." Unlike many American whites, who jump into the conversation whether invited or not, these high-context people were taught to raise their hands to speak and to wait to be recognized before joining the conversation. Since they were not invited, they felt that it was a waste of time to come, sit, and listen. They didn't feel their opinions were valued. They felt excluded.

I shared this with some of the committee chairpersons. The next time our Filipino members were nominated to serve, our chairpersons knew how to invite them into the conversation and ensure these members of color felt included. We received some wonderful questions and ideas.

The following diagram shows what systemic racism might look like in the church.

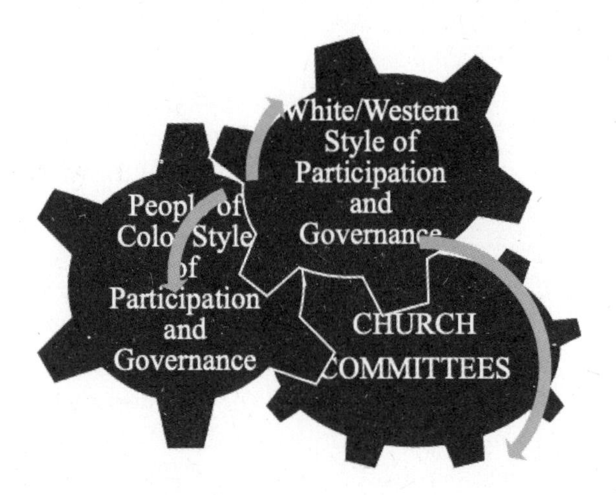

In the church I pastored, even though the Filipino members could communicate and take responsibility to share their difficulties or cultural perspectives with the white majority members and leaders, often-times those in the minority may not feel they can voice their concerns. "Respect for authority," "upbringing under hierarchal power structures," "cultural upbringing," and even "gratitude of being able to worship with the white congregation" prevents them from sharing. Some may not feel they have the "right" to say anything, unless they are asked.

For good church people, systemic racism is invisible. Systemic racism is power and privilege with prejudice (bias assumptions). Often it is seen as "just the way we always do things" or "the right way to do things." We don't realize how "our ways" can include or exclude others. "Why don't 'they' just say something?" Since the power lies with the whites in the church, it is gracious and sensitive that the whites are willing to "listen" and "make the changes" to include a "minority ethnic group" in their congregation. The congregation countered the invisible systemic racism that existed in the church.

See chapter 24, "Reality Check," "Systemic Racism: The Frog in the Kettle," "Internalized Racism," "Interrelational Racism," "Institutional Racism," and the exercises "What Happens When You Can't Believe Something to Be True?", "Resistance—What Is It?", and "Institutional and Structural Racism," online.

CHAPTER 25

The Invisible People of Color

Another example of institutional racism is the "invisibility" of Asian Americans, Pacific Islanders, and Native Americans. These populations in America have historically and traditionally been "invisible," ignored, or disregarded.

An example of this is when newly elected President Joe Biden presented candidates for his cabinet, and not one Asian American or Pacific Islander was nominated, after an East Indian, Neera Tanden, dropped out. When Senators Tammy Duckworth and Mazie Hirono vowed to vote no on any "non-diversity nominees" until Asian Americans or Pacific Islanders were appointed or nominated to high-level positions, they were told by staff that Asian Americans and Pacific Islanders had Vice-President Kamala Harris, who is half black and half Asian American. In other words, "Your people have the *one.*" Senators Duckworth and Hirono were insulted by the implication that one person of color can represent an entire racial or ethnic group.

In another incident, addressing the increase of hate crimes against Asian Americans and Pacific Islanders during the COVID-19 pandemic,[1] Asian Americans were blamed for the virus. A four-member panel of experts (three whites and one black) on NBC's *Meet the Press* discussed the concern, but not one Asian American or Pacific Islander expert was present to address violence against Asian Americans and Pacific Islanders. By the way, the host was also white.

This example serves as a reminder of this country's history. For example, when the transcontinental railroad was completed and a photograph was taken of the celebration at Promontory Summit, Utah, on May 10, 1869, not one Chinese was in the picture. Chinese people were there but were excluded from the picture. Central Pacific had hired fifteen thousand workers, more than thirteen thousand of whom were Chinese immigrants. These immigrants were paid less than white workers, and, unlike whites, had to provide their own lodging.

Native Americans and Alaska Natives have also been largely invisible. Native Americans are given fewer opportunities to be on television and in movies. The hardships and high death rates of Native Americans and Alaska Natives as a result of COVID-19 laid bare the years of neglect on Indian reservations. The lack of running water, food insecurity, and access to health care were publicly exposed during the pandemic for the rest of America to see. Added to this, four out of five Native American and Alaska Native women have experienced violence, with one in two experiencing sexual violence. If the perpetrator is a non-Native American, even if that person is the spouse of a Native American woman and living on a reservation, United States law prohibits the Native tribes from any criminal authority over non-Native Americans. In other words, only federal and state authorities can arrest and prosecute the perpetrators. The majority of persons (96 percent) committing sexual violence against Native women have been non-Native.

In addition, federal and state authorities are failing Native Americans and Alaska Natives. Between 2005 and 2009, US attorneys did not prosecute 67 percent of the cases referred to them regarding crimes of sexual abuse, nor were many even investigated.[2]

These are a few examples of the invisibility of Asian Americans, Pacific Islanders, and Native Americans.

The Model Minority Myth

Daniel Dae Kim, an Asian American actor, producer, and activist, made this statement: "Despite this disparity of experience, we continue to be tagged 'the model minority.' We simply cannot continue to live with the myth that the most successful of us represents the totality of us."

The model minority myth is dangerous because it is a stereotype that places Asian Americans, in particular, "above" and "opposed" to other people of color. The myth is used against other people of color to say, "Why can't you people be like the Asian Americans who are successful, doing well, and have no complaints!"

When conducting my cross-cultural research in South Carolina, one of the churches I was assigned to interview was a small, rural, white church with a newly appointed Korean pastor. The district superintendent told me that they could never have appointed a black clergyperson to that church. "Koreans are honorary whites down here, so this appointment will be accepted." —Shan

However, Koreans being accepted in general as honorary whites and the myth of Asian superiority do not reflect reality. Asian Americans are not a monolithic ethnic group. There are huge disparities among Asian Americans. Some Asian Americans (e.g., Japanese, Chinese, East Indians, some Filipinos, and Koreans) have been in this country for generations and have been able to build stable, middle- and upper-class lives here, in spite of discrimination. But there also are more recent immigrants and refugees who are living below the poverty line (e.g., Nepalese, Hmong, Laotian, Burmese, Korean, and Pakistani).

And in more recent decades, those allowed into the United States (other than for family reunification) have been students, professionals, and skilled workers, not ordinary laborers (unlike the unskilled laborers in the past). Many of the newer immigrants already come with resources.

The model minority myth makes Asian Americans invisible. If they are doing well, they don't have needs, they don't need help, and they don't matter in the discussion of race. The false belief persists that Asian Americans do not face discrimination and racism.

The model minority myth has some in America believing that Asian Americans belong in the "white" category. Placing them there ignores the past—and current—history of racism against Asian Americans. Some Americans were even caught by surprise when increased violence against Asian Americans occurred during the COVID-19 pandemic. (Asian Americans weren't surprised!)

Our government had made it clear that Asian Americans were not "white" in laws that prevented Asian Americans from citizenship. It was a Chinese American who fought against the US government in the courts for "birthright citizenship in 1898" and won. Up until then, persons could be born in the US, but if they were of a certain ethnicity, they could not become a citizen.

The reality is that Asian Americans are not white and do not have the privilege and power of whites in America.

Questions to Ponder . . .

1. What are the messages given to Asian Americans, Pacific Islanders, and Native Americans about their value and significance in this country?
2. Why do you think these populations in the United States are so "invisible"?
3. How does institutional racism play into their "invisibility"?

4. How has the model minority myth hurt Asian Americans?
5. How has the model minority myth caused tension among Asian Americans and people of color?
6. How does the model minority myth advantage whites in America? Think about the ways this myth can cause animosity and disunity among people of color while leaving white America off the hook.

NOTES

1. During the first year-and-a-half of the COVID-19 pandemic, more than a 150 percent increase in hate crimes against Asian Americans and Pacific Islanders were reported, including cases of harassment, abuse, violence, and killing.

2. See "Ending Violence Against Native Women," Indian Law Resource Center, https://indianlaw.org/issue/ending-violence-against-native-women.

CHAPTER 26

Microaggressions Are a Macro Problem

My cousin recently recounted this story: "My mother and aunt took my sister and my cousin to a beauty college when the girls were about four and five years old, respectively. The students had not cut Asian hair before, so the teacher told the whole class to come on over to my sister and cousin to touch and feel their hair. My cousin remembered thinking, 'What the heck. Are we that weird?'"
—Katie

Microaggressions are comments, questions, or actions that are unconscious or unintentional but reflect prejudicial attitudes toward a target group. Taken over time, with consistency, microaggressions are harmful to the target group in two ways. First, they increase internalized racism when one begins to believe the prejudicial attitudes about oneself. Second, they cement the prejudicial attitude of the non-target person, who then believes these microaggressions to be the truth. This becomes a macro problem because it affects all of society. Microaggressions can lead to attitudes about people of color affecting their treatment in health care, policing and criminal justice, media portrayals, employment, education, government assistance and programs, financial institutions, or housing. The following are some examples of spoken microaggressions for multiracial persons. Review these along with the online resources that can help us think critically about our spoken words and actions and how they may affect a person of color (see chapter 26 online for an exercise and the chart "Microaggressions and Their Messages"). This can help us stop ourselves from perpetuating microaggressions or at the least ask a person of color if what was just said was a microaggression.

A funny twist . . . at the US Consulate in Guangzhou, China, one of the white officers complained that the Chinese people made him feel uncomfortable and like he didn't belong, that he stood out, and on top of that, they kept touching his daughter's blonde hair. The Chinese Americans, his colleagues, looked at him and said, "Welcome to our lives. We get that every day in the US!" —Katie

Microaggressions and Multiracial People

The number of multiracial people in the United States has been growing. More than ten million people self-identified as multiracial in 2018, the majority residing in the western part of the United States. Multiracial Americans also experience racism and microaggressions. The following are some microaggressive statements or questions experienced by multiracial people.

"What are you?" This question implies oddity and difference. (This question is also asked of non-black and non-white persons, such as Asian Americans, in trying to figure out one's Asian heritage.) The person asking this question tries to put multiracial people into acceptable "racial boxes."

"Okay, but are you more black or white?" This again tries to put multiracial people into a box, forcing an either/or, because a person "cannot" be both.

"Choose the one you're most of." This oft-heard response given to students taking standardized tests and struggling to fill in a required racial category forces multiracial students to have to choose only one part of their identity.

"How did your parents meet? Is your father in the military?" The assumption is that interracial marriages happen because military men are exposed to women from other countries. Also, there is an implied belief that military men "fool around" and women from other countries are either "loose" or want to marry an American to gain citizenship.

"You don't look _____________." This comment implies that a person has to fit a stereotypical look of a certain ethnic group. If you are multiracial, you might not fit that "look." You are strange.

"Are you adopted?" This implies that you look different from your parents or siblings. Your skin color stands out. You can't possibly belong to your birth family; therefore, you must have been adopted.

"You're so exotic!" This is saying you are not normal like everyone else.

My teenage children felt very nervous when we, as a multiracial family, were eating in a restaurant because they noticed that people were staring at us. Some microaggressions can be nonverbal.
—Shan

"You're not black enough." This indicates that you don't belong with the black community, even though you are part black. (This statement doesn't recognize that many African Americans descended from enslaved ancestors who were raped by their white masters and therefore have white or European DNA in them.) The implication is that because one has "lighter skin" one can "pass" and have more privilege than darker blacks. However, to the white community, this person is seen as black.

My daughter, who is black/white, attended some social meetings where participants met in groups. When she tried to join an African American women's group, they did not respect her. They told her she was "not really black." She didn't talk right; she didn't walk right. She said she was disgusted and hurt, and she reported to me that "I don't need them; I know who I am." —Shan

"Where are you really from?" The person asking can't believe you are an American. Americans don't look like you. (This is also asked of non-black and white persons, especially Latinx, Asian Americans, and Pacific Islanders, indicating they cannot be true Americans but must be foreigners.)

"Can I take a picture with you?" This question objectifies a multiracial person. You are so strange and "alien" that a person would want to show you off to his or her family and friends.

"Can I touch your hair?" Again, you are different, exotic, strange. They can't believe you exist, so they have to touch you.

"Where'd you get your kids from?" People can't believe your kids are "your kids" because they all look so different from one another (e.g., skin color). Never mind that other parts of the kids and you look like each other (eyes, nose, mouth, etc.).

I have two black/white children and one East Indian child. When my children were very young and I was out with them, I was asked, "Oh, do you run a daycare?" —Shan

Questions to Ponder . . .

Think about any multiracial family members or friends you have. Or if you are multiracial yourself or married to a person of another ethnicity, think about your experience.

1. What remarks or questions have you or your multiracial family and friends been asked that surprised you or them or made you or them uncomfortable?

2. How did you or they respond to these remarks or questions? Did you or they like the way it was handled? If not, what would you or they do differently?
3. If you desire to build relationships with those who don't understand multiracial marriages or people, what are some ways you might try to help their understanding?
4. Why do you think it is important for Americans to understand multiracial Americans?

PART 6

MORE THAN BRIDGE BUILDING

Becoming an Ally

Rev. Dr. Dale M. Weatherspoon

CHAPTER 27

Building a Structure for a Beloved Community

The anthropologist invited the children from an African tribe to play one game. He placed a basket of fruit near the tree and announced, addressing the children: "The one of you who reaches the tree first will be rewarded with all of the sweet fruits." When he signaled to the children to start the race, they locked their hands tightly and ran together, and then they all sat together and enjoyed the delicious fruit.

The astonished anthropologist asked the children why they all ran together, because each of them could have enjoyed the fruit for himself or herself, to which the children replied: "Obonato," "Obonato," or "Ubuntu," which in their language means, "I exist because we exist." "Is it possible for one to be happy if everyone else is sad?" —Traditional African Folklore

The Importance of Relationships

We are created to be in relationship with one another. Lack of relationships and healthy connections leads to isolation and depression. The challenges of the pandemic in the year 2020 showed us the importance of relationships, both personal and systemic.

God didn't just create Adam. God also created Eve so that the two could have companionship and be in relationship with one another and with God. Companionship provided each with someone to talk with, someone who could listen as the other shared his or her thoughts, dreams, hurts, and pains, as well as their joys and celebrations. Companionship provided help-mates to one another, making daily life a little easier and life's challenges a bit more bearable. Companionship was also a source of encouragement when the road got difficult.

The coronavirus pandemic has shown our interconnectedness with and interdependence on one another. We depended on essential workers, whether at the supermarkets, the hospitals, or the banks. We looked forward to receiving our mail, mostly. We are thankful when the beauty parlors and barbershops are open. We are grateful that our police officers and firefighters respond when called. We don't need walls that separate and divide us. We need to strengthen the bridges we have and build more bridges to connect us. As we heard throughout the year 2020, we are all in this together!

During the COVID-19 pandemic, NBA star Stephen Curry collaborated with the Bruce Lee Foundation to respond to anti-Asian acts of hatred by designing custom-made basketball shoes picturing Bruce Lee and his family with the quote, "Under the heavens, there is but one family." The shoes were auctioned and the proceeds were given to families of the Atlanta-area Asian victims who were shot in March 2021. Shannon Lee, the daughter of Bruce Lee, said the gift of the shoes was "a beautiful example of allyship and solidarity in action."

Healthy relationships and working together for the well-being of our communities impact us physically and emotionally. Great things can be accomplished when we work together. For example, people working together increased the voter turnout across the United States for the 2020 elections. People working together to achieve a dream can change established traditions and systems for the better.

When I began taking accordion lessons from a teacher in the North Beach section of San Francisco, the Saturday bus rides from my neighborhood to his studio were interesting. Like a dance, there was a rhythm to the ride. When I boarded the bus, a mixture of people—blacks, whites, and Chinese—were among the riders. As the bus continued its route, more blacks boarded. When we came to the stop where the local train station was located, more white people from the peninsula coming into the city to shop boarded the bus. The ride from there was about a mile to downtown. At the downtown Market Street stop, everybody seemed to disembark except the Chinese and me. More Chinese boarded. Although many Italians lived in North Beach, Chinatown was close by. The North Beach sights, sounds (language), smells, and customs introduced me to the diverse city where I lived. —Dale

When we are not in right relationship with God and with one another (the other being our neighbor or those who are different from us in any way), healthy relationships are broken. Systemic racism is not healthy for individuals, communities, or our nation. We have seen how a bad water system in Michigan has affected people of color more than the white population. We have seen during Hurricane Katrina how people of color and poor folks living on the flat ground were disproportionately impacted more than those living at higher elevations and farther away from the river. Systemic racism leads to more people of color being incarcerated and murdered by law enforcement officials. All of us pay the cost for these systemic sins, and some more than others. We need to accurately diagnose the illness to bring about a proper and effective cure. We need a vaccination for this virus called racism and white supremacy. The Scriptures tell us that when one suffers, we all suffer, and when one rejoices, we all rejoice. It is time for the suffering caused by systemic racism, prejudice, stereotyping, and lying to end.

More on Becoming a Bridge Person

Again, what is a bridge person? Like a bridge that connects two places, a bridge person is someone who can connect two or more cultures. A bridge person is someone who understands and is sensitive to different cultures and can bring people in these different cultures together. He or she is a person who can provide guidance and expertise in understanding between the cultures. So how can we become a bridge person? (See the exercise "Learning About and Appreciating a Culture," chapter 27, online.)

Humankind has not woven the web of life. We are but one thread within it. Whatever we do to the web, we do to ourselves. All things are bound together. All things connect. —Chief Seattle

CHAPTER 28

Moving Toward a Beloved Community

We hate each other because we fear each other. And we fear each other because we do not know each other. And we do not know each other because we are separated from each other.
—Rev. Dr. Martin Luther King Jr.

The movement toward becoming a Beloved Community and a person who is interculturally sensitive takes time, patience, and progressive steps. What are the stages of progression from a monocultural mindset to an intercultural mindset?

Dr. Milton Bennett, an American sociologist, has provided the Developmental Model of Intercultural Sensitivity (DMIS). In this model, on p. 133, Dr. Bennett helps us understand the progression from seeing our own culture as central to seeing our role or behavior in different cultural contexts. The six stages of progression are denial, polarization or defense, minimization, acceptance, adaptation, and integration.

Let's explore each progressive stage. Now, one caution we want to give is that these stages may not take place in a linear fashion. Like most of life, as we grow in understanding the things

Developmental Model of Intercultural Sensitivity

denial	defense	minimization	acceptance	adaptation	integration
Seeing Your Culture as Central			Seeing Behavior in a Cultural Context		

(Ethnocentrism) → **(Ethnorelativism)**

we experience, we can also lapse into earlier behavior and understanding from time to time. An illustration of a rubber band helps explain this concept. As we grow, our world expands, and we are stretched in our understanding of life. However, just like a rubber band, when the stretched band is let go, it snaps back toward its original shape. Yet, it never quite goes back to the actual original shape because it has been stretched. This can go on and on until the rubber band is completely stretched. (Now, let's not go too far in this analogy, because a rubber band stretched too much can break.)

Denial

In the denial stage, we are disinterested or avoid differences we have with other cultures. We keep ourselves away from people who are different from us. We may do this on purpose or unconsciously. We isolate or separate ourselves from "those others."

In the early 1970s I was a lay volunteer working in a Chinese American church. It was right after the Civil Rights Act of 1964, and many of us were working on breaking down walls of racism. Our church leaders joined sister church relationships with a white church and a black church. We decided to bring the youth groups of our church and the black church together, so we invited the black church youth to come to San Francisco Chinatown to have dinner and fellowship. Our youth and leaders prepared the dinner, and as the black youth came into the church and sat, ready for our dinner, I noticed that not one of our youth was around. They had disappeared when dinner was about to be served. What happened? I was embarrassed and angry at our youth. They had left. The leaders ended up serving dinner and having fellowship with the black youth. The next day was Sunday, and we confronted our youth. Why did they run off? Our youth explained that they were scared. They were afraid of the black youth. None of them had any friends who were black, and many had very little association with blacks. They had grown up isolated and didn't feel the need to associate with blacks. Needless to say, we began a vigorous spiritual and educational process with our youth. —Katie

Defense

In the defense stage, we recognize that there are cultural differences, but we view these differences negatively. We have an "us" and "them" attitude. We feel our culture is better or superior. We look down on the other cultures. We "defend" our culture against the other cultures.

In the 1970s, our denomination, American Baptists, began a program called Fund of Renewal. One of the goals of the program was to encourage local churches to relate to each other interculturally. As one of the leaders of this program in our church, I visited a white church in a rural community for a cultural exchange. At the time, one of the hot topics in our state elections was bilingual education. Already, a number of schools had begun immersion programs in which elementary school children were learning more than one language, starting as early as kindergarten. As I shared my excitement with members of the rural, white congregation regarding these immersion programs and how the children were becoming bilingual, a teacher in the rural church challenged me. She believed that children should learn only one language; otherwise, they would be all mixed up. And that one language should be English, the official language of the country, and the most important language. She saw no need for children to be bilingual in an increasingly globally connected world. English would do just fine. The rest of the world can learn English. To her, English was the superior language, and America was the best country in the world. Period.

This is defense played out in real life.

Of course, I countered her with the argument that children can learn languages easier than we adults. Children in many European countries know multiple languages and can navigate well among different cultures. Swiss children can speak English, German, and French. And I believe that our American children are just as smart as the Swiss! —Katie

Minimization

Minimization is the stage where many individuals and most churches live. Eric Law, an intercultural consultant and founder of the Kaleidoscope Institute, asserts that minimization is the greatest block to true inclusion in the church. Through minimization, we view others as basically the same as us or like us. We believe that we all operate on the same basic set of values. All human beings are essentially the same. The differences are minimal.

Because this is the stage the majority of people are in and most comfortable with, let's look at minimization in more detail.

My research project, which focused on clergy who were pastoring congregations that were ethnically and/or racially different than the clergyperson, was based on interviews with clergy and discussion with focus groups composed of lay persons in the congregation. Two of the settings were totally white congregations with African-American clergymen. One was in an affluent suburb of a major city and the other was in the major city of a predominately rural area surrounded by oil fields. Both were large congregations by United Methodist standards of the area.

The neighborhood near the suburban congregation had been changing, becoming racially diverse. The leaders had specifically requested that an African-American clergy be assigned as an associate pastor to facilitate and guide the congregation in reaching out into that changing neighborhood. The clergyperson who was assigned had diverse urban experiences, an ideal match, it would seem.

The clergyperson shared with me that he was surprised that the church leaders had never asked him about his experiences as a black man, which would be relevant to their goal of community outreach. Knowing this, when I held the focus group with the laypersons, one of the questions I asked was, "What have you learned from Rev. __________ about his growing up black that will be helpful in your outreach?" The room became deathly silent; as they say, you could hear a pin drop. Finally, one brave woman said, "But wouldn't it be prejudiced to ask him that, to ask him about being black?"

My response was that I personally didn't think so; however, I suggested that they ask him if it would be all right to talk with him about that. I was sure he would not be offended and would give them a thoughtful answer.

This was a major learning experience for me, one I had not anticipated. It seemed to me, upon reflection, that pointing out that

the clergy was black was assumed to be a negative, disrespectful act or a microaggression. How could that be, I wondered, since he was obviously black. He knew he was black! As I continued to ponder, it dawned on me that the assumption in mainstream values was that being white was the natural, good, and right way to be. Therefore, to be black was to be deviant in some essential fashion. I do not mean to imply that the lay person thought this consciously; in fact, she would have undoubtedly denied having such thoughts. However, I can't make sense of it in any other way. With that understanding it would be rude or disrespectful to point out a trait that is judged to be negative. Therefore, one must minimize the difference and pretend not to notice. The sad irony is that by so doing the laypersons lost the very resource they were seeking.
—Shan

Questions to Ponder . . .

1. Share this story with another person or in a small group.
2. Let's take a few minutes to reflect on the question of why the layperson might have the concern about being perceived as prejudiced.
3. Discuss together what answers and/or questions come up. Do this without judgment, not asking "why" questions but rather to gain more insight or information about the thinking processes people were using.
4. Finally, reflect together or individually on the ways you have experienced these concerns. How did you respond?

Acceptance

In the acceptance stage, we recognize and appreciate cultural differences, and we see the complexities of difference.

My youngest son attended a church-based preschool. One of the enrichment programs was called "Innovative." The classroom was set up to represent the world; even the rug was a map of the world. Once a week, the students would learn about different countries and talk about the different customs and cultures. The preschool invited parents from different cultures to come in and share with the children. Parents would come dressed in clothing from their country or culture. Music and food were also shared. The dolls the children played with were of different ethnicities. There was even a basket of ladies' nylon stockings in different colors. The children could place the nylon stockings on their arms to simulate changing skin colors. What a great way for children to learn about a diverse world. —Dale

Adaptation and Integration

As we grow in our acceptance, we begin to adapt. In the *adaptation* stage, we are developing skills that are becoming more of "natural" behavior in more than one culture. We develop empathy and can begin to see from the other's perspective.

In the *integration* stage, we have a sense of self that can move in and out of different cultures. We can maintain our original identity and be comfortable in any culture. We can also be on the "margins" of any culture, having the ability to see many perspectives. This stage is hard to reach without immersion in another culture. Adaptation is the goal. For more on these see chapter 28, the online additions "A Colorblind White Congregation with a Black Pastor," "Adaptation," "Integration," the "Developmental Model of Intercultural Sensitivity Exercise," and "Next Steps."

CHAPTER 29

Intentionality in Building Relationships

Great results don't just happen. You have to be intentional.
—Michael Hyatt

When visiting a church that was predominantly white in the Midwest, I was greeted at the door by a smiling white man. He asked me where I was from and whether I was Chinese. I said yes. He then said there was a Chinese church down the street, and that I might be more comfortable there because they spoke my "language." I said I only spoke English. —Katie

How do we break this pattern? What actions can we take so that our churches become more diverse like the places where many work each day? What if white people invite people of color to their churches? Could people of color invite white people to their churches? Perhaps people of one ethnic group invite people of another ethnic group? And not just invite, but accompany them so that when they arrive at the church they do not feel alone? Accompanying them would let others know the guest is not lost or in the wrong place, as mentioned in the real-life story from Katie, or as often happens when a black person walks through the doors of a white church alone. Accompanying the person of color would be a sign to the white members that this person is your friend. Whether it is a person of color bringing a white person to the church, a white person bringing a person of color to the church, or a person of color bringing a person of a different ethnicity to the church, sitting with him or her would make the guest feel more comfortable. Instead of feeling lost, the guest would have a personal tour guide to direct him or her through the traditions and liturgy of the church, such as when to stand and when to sit.

Target Visualization

Did you ever watch *Star Trek*? The first television series began in 1966, and now there are numerous television series and movies based on the Star Trek genre. What made Star Trek unique was the science it was based on and how the writers used their imaginations to visualize the future. A number of their imagined technologies and inventions have now become a reality. We were first introduced to handheld communicators (the flip phone), universal translators (translations now available on our smartphones), speaking to computers (Siri, Cortana, OK Google, anyone?), wireless earpieces (like today's Bluetooth), sliding doors (ubiquitous now in many buildings), food replicators (3D printers), holodeck (virtual reality), and Personal Access Display Devices or PADD (readers and tablet computers).

Imagining or visualizing what could be shapes how we see reality and thus affects our expectations, hopes, behavior, and often outcomes. It can play a role in our decision-making. Think about the 2020 presidential election. What role did imagination play in how people voted and how people perceived the outcome of the election?

One way to help ourselves break out of the pattern of systemic racism is to visualize ourselves breaking out. Can we visualize how we can overcome the different aspects of systemic racism . . . internal, interpersonal, and institutional? In other words, if we can imagine ourselves overcoming and defeating racism, could we then see ourselves doing so in real life?

Frank Borman, commander of the Apollo 8 mission, put it this way: "When you're finally up at the moon looking back on Earth, all those differences and nationalistic traits are pretty well going to blend, and you're going to get a concept that maybe this really is one world, and why the hell can't we learn to live together like decent people?"

Can we imagine a different world? A different future?

One way of doing this is to practice target visualization. First, we think of ourselves as targets. We realize that everyone has been targeted for mistreatment and everyone has resisted the best way they can at some point in their lives. We are not talking about degrees or who is worse off than anyone else. However, generally speaking, at some period of our lives, we have been mistreated by someone else. Remember a time when that happened. This can aid a person in understanding and empathizing with others since they too have been targets sometime in their lives. And it helps people see how one can be an advocate or an ally in these situations. Sometimes thinking back to a particular incident can help a person be less self-blaming or ashamed regarding their part in that incident. The incident might involve something said or done to them, publicly or privately, overtly or subtly. Who was doing the mistreatment? Who was there? Where were you at the time? What was said or done? What was the person's tone of voice who mistreated you? What did he or she look like? What did it feel like for you? What were your thoughts? How have these feelings and thoughts stayed with you? What changed for you after this experience? How did you resist this mistreatment? Resistance could be through actions, thoughts, words, emotions, art, music, writing, and religion, among other things.

Now imagine that if someone from the same group as the person mistreating you could have intervened. What would this person say or do? How would your resistance be different if this advocate or ally was there to help? How might you be an advocate or ally for a targeted person today?

Non-Target Visualization

In systemic racism, not only have we been targets, but also there are times in our lives we have been in a non-target group. In other words, we have learned misinformation, stereotypes, and prejudices about target groups. Sometimes what we have learned is buried so deep, normalized, and rationalized that we may have trouble recognizing it.

Try to remember a time when you have been taught something about a target group by someone from your own group. Who was teaching? Who else was there at the time? Where were you? What was said or done? What was the involved person's tone of voice? What did she, he, or they look like? What were your feelings and thoughts during this experience? How have these feelings and thoughts stayed with you? What changed for you after this experience? Did you want to resist these teachings? If so, how? This could be through emotions, actions, thoughts, words, art, music, writing, and religion. Imagine if someone from your own racial or ethnic group intervened. What would you have wanted that person to say or do?

How would that have changed your thoughts and actions today? (See chapter 29, "Becoming a Bridge Person," online.)

CHAPTER 30

Personal Commitment and Action Plan

There's a children's fairy tale about the tortoise and the hare. They were in a race, and of course the hare was a lot faster than the tortoise. The hare knew it, was arrogant about it, and even touted it against the tortoise during the race. During the race, the hare was so far ahead of the tortoise, and so confident that he could win, he decided he didn't need to hurry, slowed down, and even took a nap. Meanwhile the tortoise just plodded along at his own pace, moving slowly toward the finish line. The hare, after his nap, decided to finish the race. However, before he knew it, the tortoise had nearly reached the finish line. The hare ran as fast as he could, but it was too late. The tortoise won!

I can imagine that the commitment to undo the shackles of systemic racism, to become a person who can resist racism, and to become anti-racist is much like that race. Some of us think that we can easily undo what we have learned from society by making friends with people of other cultures, diversifying our areas of employment, inviting differing peoples to become members of our churches, eating ethnic foods and listening to ethnic music, learning the intercultural buzz words, participating in diversity training, reading books or watching movies about racism, and so on. We are like the hare in some ways. We might think we've got this race in the bag, so to speak.

In reality, the race toward ending systemic racism's influence on us is more at the pace of the tortoise. It is slow; it is steady; it is patiently peeling the onion, as someone put it.

Choosing to relate to people who are very different from us and, particularly, choosing to go against systemic racism will not be easy. It can take a lifetime of painstakingly dismantling preconceived thought processes, attitudes, and ideas. It will be hard. But it will be well worth it, not only for those who have been victims of prejudice, discrimination, and racism, but also for those who have benefitted from systemic racism.

So how do we begin this process of dismantling racism and being anti-racist personally?

Before being the pastor of Allen Temple, I worked for the M&M Board as a Western Field Representative. For my sabbatical, they sent me to Cuernavaca, Mexico, to study Spanish and Hispanic culture with Father Ivan Illich at El Centro del Cultural, which trained missionaries and others to serve in Spanish-speaking settings.

Local pastors like the late John Garcia of San Francisco, and Vahac Mardirosian tutored me. I preached in Spanish the eulogy of the mother of the Reverend Ruben Hurtado, founding pastor and emeritus of Iglesias Bautista de Allen Temple. This ministry was established in March 1992, and the Reverend Isai Hurtado is the present pastor. The church now owns its own property two blocks from ATBC on International Blvd.

Isai follows his father as pastor, who served twenty-three years and planted Allen Temple Church in El Salvador with a woman pastor, Sarah Gavay Martinez . . . —Rev. Dr. J. Alfred Smith Sr.

Rev. Smith's journey toward being intercultural was a gradual and intentional process. Being a Black American, he chose to relate to the Latinx communities in California and in particular in the neighborhood surrounding his church. It was step by step, from learning Spanish to helping a Hispanic church become established. Rev. Smith is one example of someone who has a growth mindset.

Fixed or Growth Mindset

Sometimes God provides an opportunity for us to grow. A Korean-American pastor shared the story of how an impromptu meeting led to a beautiful intercultural relationship. When he and his family first immigrated to the United States (to one of the Southern states) and were getting acquainted with their new surroundings, they ran across a nice city park with a large banner that read, "Lee Family Reunion Picnic." They were so excited, thinking that they may have found some long-lost relatives or, at least, fellow Korean immigrants. They parked their car and headed toward the reunion, but when they arrived, they were so surprised to see that the Lee family was African American! When the African American Lees found out who the Korean family was, they warmly welcomed the Koreans as part of their new Lee family. The Korean Lees continued the relationship after that chance encounter and kept going to the black family's reunions. —Katie

One thing we can do is to work on our mindset. To be open to new opportunities for growth, we need to ask ourselves, Do we have a fixed mindset or a growth mindset? Or do we have a mixture of both? Which areas do we need to work on? Rosetta Eun Ryong Lee, an educator and diversity consultant for Seattle Girls' School in Seattle, Washington, developed a table that compares the two mindsets. The fixed mindset hinders our ability to become anti-racist or go against the confines of systemic racism, while a growth mindset helps us overcome the influences and power of racism.

Another way of having a growth mindset is to think "outside the box." Do you know how Velcro was invented? George de Mestral in the 1940s was hunting in the Swiss mountains when he realized that the tiny hooks of the cockle-burs kept getting stuck on his pants and his dog's fur. He wondered how they attached themselves. Under the microscope he observed the hooks engaging the loops in his pants' fabric. Now, many of us would have just seen these cockle-burs as a nuisance and a pain to take off our clothes. George de Mestral saw otherwise!

What if we can see how we can overcome and resist racism with fresh eyes? (See chapter 30, "21-Day Racial Equity Habit Building Challenge" and "Two Mindsets Toward Cultural Competency," online.)

CHAPTER 31

Enlisting My Church

If you really want to make a friend, go to someone's house and eat with him . . . The people who give you their food give you their heart. —Cesar Chavez

Partner with Sister Churches

Another way to intentionally build relationships is for one church to partner with a culturally different church. That partnership can be across denominational, socioeconomic, political, or ethnic lines. Exchanging pastors or choirs helps to educate each congregation about different styles of worship. Worshiping together in each other's buildings means each one is giving something up while benefitting from the opportunity to experience a different style and tradition of worship. Feelings of discomfort will probably arise from this experience, but the result will be a powerful opportunity to grow and celebrate.

In an effort to bridge the racial or ethnic divide, build relationships, and remove some of the fear and myths, my Methodist congregation formed a partnership with a Lutheran congregation in a neighboring city. After the Lutheran pastor spoke at a Good Friday service at my church, she and I had lunch together.

We came up with the idea of a joint worship service. After that, the Lutheran congregation came to worship with our Methodist church, and the Lutheran pastor preached. A joint choir from both churches shared a musical selection in the morning service, and one of their Sunday school teachers led the Children's Moment. After the service, we shared in a fellowship time. On another Sunday, our Methodist congregation worshiped with the Lutheran church. Again, we had a joint choir, and one of our Sunday school teachers led the Children's Moment. I preached. After the worship service, we had a wonderful potluck where members were encouraged to get acquainted by sitting with someone from the other congregation. In addition, after the service, we worked together on a service project. We bagged meals for those in the community with need. It was a delightful exchange. Excitement and joy abounded when members realized they were neighbors or had been employed in the same workplace or were connected in some other ways. Working side by side on the service project helped us to realize we were in ministry together.

Unfortunately, for several reasons, the relationship didn't last long. For one, the Lutheran pastor held an interim position, and she was not sure how long she would be at her church. Second, time and intentional work are required to nurture a relationship. And third, more preparation was needed to nurture the relationship. Having a small committee from each church dialoguing around a vision and sustained purpose would have been helpful and productive. Though the partnership didn't last, I believe some good seeds were planted in both congregations.

Find Common Ministries

Another opportunity to build intentional bridges is through interfaith and ecumenical work. Many communities invite faith-based organizations to participate in ministries for the homeless and hungry. Local jails invite faith-based organizations to visit those who are incarcerated or to come and teach classes such as a Bible study, art, poetry writing, or English as a second language. Many cities have interfaith councils. I have found these to be a great way to learn about other faith traditions, what they believe, and how they live and serve. I always appreciate the differences while acknowledging what we have in common. These encounters lead me to want to learn more and deepen relationships with others not like me.

Forming an Inclusive Group[1]

How do we start to build intentional bridges and make a difference in our communities? We begin by being inclusive and finding intercultural partnerships. All too often, groups organized to make their communities a better place to live are made up of members of only one racial or ethnic group. Or all the initiating, planning, and organizing is done by one racial or ethnic group. Others are invited, but leadership and direction are never shared. How can we be sure of full participation and not have one racial or ethnic group dominate?

The following four steps can help you form planning committees that include many of the diverse groups in your city or region. First, you can state clearly the reasons for inclusiveness. Second, identify and invite leaders in preparation for a major event or community service you wish to plan. Third, get acquainted and plan the event or community service. Fourth, once you develop an inclusive group, keep it going.

State Your Reasons for Becoming More Inclusive

One reason for inclusive planning is that God loves the entire world and all the people whom God has created. Loving as God loves means respecting the identity, worth, and distinct life experiences and history of each person.

Second, in a genuine community, each person has a say in decisions affecting the well-being of the community. Following the practice of the earliest church in Acts, participative planning is essential. Those without a say in planning will not own the results of it.

Third, inclusiveness means seeing common concerns. Each group, as well as each individual within the group, will have particular concerns and agendas. Each will speak from his or her own perspective and will tend to define his or her problems their own way. Only as these positions are stated will it be possible for leaders to see connections between diverse agendas and concerns. Listening leads to being able to see what may be good for everyone.

Fourth, movement toward the good of all starts when everyone begins to speak and work together. As community leaders know, coalition building is the key to effectiveness. No group or person finally makes it on their own. Changes for the better in policies and practices of agencies, corporations, and governmental bodies require a coordinated effort.

Identify and Invite Leaders

Identify major groupings that might be included (gender, race, ethnicity, class). Decide how wide a net you and your group are going to be able to cast. No matter how well-intentioned and effective you are, it will usually be impossible to include leaders of all of the diverse groups in your community.

Contact leaders of groups well in advance. Ask persons you know from a given group to recommend somebody: "We are going to be doing a retreat; would you recommend somebody who can help us plan it?" If you have no contacts with a given group, call a minister from the group or write an email or letter to such a person. You might get in touch with a group like the NAACP or others that would have such contacts. Church Women United often has contacts with diverse groups. If there is a local community organization or regional association of community organizations, they also would have names of persons with whom you can be in touch. Your regional denominational offices may have lists of ministers and laypersons who would possibly come to such a meeting—so might the Ministers Alliance, Council of Churches, and other such bodies.

Choose a place for your meeting that is not narrowly identified with some particular group's turf. A pleasant and attractive neutral location is a good place to begin.

Once you have the names of some contact persons, you may call, email, or write a letter. You may ask for recommendations of persons to attend your planning meeting. Be sure to express your hope for such a partnership.

Some people will probably respond. Talk to them in person or by phone. Get their names and addresses. Find out who recommended them, extend the invitation to attend your meeting, and be clear about the time, place, and how to get there.

Get Acquainted and Plan the Event or Community Service

You have contacted prospective members of your planning committee well in advance. You have explained the reason that you are meeting. On the day of your meeting, you will end up with a somewhat diverse planning committee. Of course, some who promised to come won't be there. You might end up with a smaller group than hoped. But that's okay. You can start small; as interest increases, participation will increase.

Begin with the reason for the planning meeting. Ask the committee members to introduce themselves, say a little bit about why they responded to the invitation, and one thing they would like to see happen.

Start each meeting with helpful get-acquainted exercises or icebreakers. Allow time for people to share their stories. Serving food is an excellent way to break the ice. You can plan on having different ethnic foods and sharing stories about the foods.

Listen! Do what you can to create a safe climate, one in which people expect that they will listen to one another and say what they are thinking and feeling. Remember that you will be overcoming the attitude that says, "I/we know what is best for everyone!" Instead, foster an attitude of recognizing that we don't know what is best for others and are willing to listen and learn. Expect that each person will speak from a different perspective. Listening and then understanding what each person is feeling will help as you continue to meet. You will have times of great agreement and times of discomfort and even misunderstanding. Prepare to take action on what each person feels is important.

Take notes. Putting things up on a flip chart pad or a whiteboard is a good way to make sure that everyone can see what is being said. Taking notes on the substance of what the group communicates is helpful and recording the group's decisions is very important. Don't only record the decisions, but also record the names of people who will accept responsibility and be accountable for the work.

After the meeting is over, review the minutes and notes and make sure a copy is sent or emailed to each person who attended the meeting. Then, decide among the participants who will be your leaders. Make sure the leaders represent the diversity of your group.

Keep Your Inclusive Movement Going

Your leaders will coordinate follow-up meetings. Within your group of leaders, prepare to meet separately and build trust. As leaders meet, deepen your understanding of the experiences, concerns, and issues affecting each person. Lift each one in support and prayer.

As your group continues to meet, discover the connections between people, the diverse racial or ethnic groups, and the complexities within each group. Be patient. Make sure you acknowledge that participants will make mistakes and sometimes might unintentionally say something or do something that may be hurtful, prejudicial, or racist. When this happens, ask for forgiveness and encourage the person offended or hurt to bring this up so everyone can learn from these mistakes. (See the intercultural sensitivity exercises in the online workbook, part 2, chapter 7.)

And when the group has accomplished its agreed-upon goal, celebrate and have a party!

Questions to Ponder . . .

1. What church, group, or organization might you want to partner with?
2. How would you go about doing that? What will be your first steps? Who could you contact?
3. What would be your purpose or goal for partnering?
4. Where do you plan to meet initially?
5. How would you ensure inclusiveness? What are some guidelines you would suggest?
6. How long would you partner together?
7. How would you define growth or progress?

See chapter 31, "Three Stories," online.

NOTES

1. Adapted from Cora Tucker and Owen D. Owens, appendix M, in Kathryn Choy-Wong, *Building Bridges: A Handbook for Cross-Cultural Ministry* (Valley Forge, PA: Judson Press, 1998).

CHAPTER 32

Being the Change in My Community

In the 1970s, hunger and homelessness were major problems in American cities. Sounds familiar? A group of hunger/homelessness organizations and church groups organized themselves into the Food Network. This Christian-based effort was sponsored by what was then called the Northern California Ecumenical Council. The purpose of the network was to help each organization in its efforts to address and stem hunger and homelessness and to make changes in the state's laws and policies to tackle these problems. The network began by pooling its resources to buy staples in bulk, such as rice, beans, powdered milk, and canned goods. This saved considerable amounts of money for each organization.

Next, the network sought to receive massive donations but found that grocery stores and restaurants weren't donating to this type of organization for fear of becoming liable and vulnerable to lawsuits if the donated foods caused people to become ill. Grocery stores continued to dump food after the expiration dates, and restaurants threw away any leftovers at the end of closing time. So, the network lobbied the state legislature to pass a Good Samaritan bill to protect grocery stores and restaurants from being liable. Once the bill was passed, massive donations began to come in. One donation came from a derailed train carrying fifty tons of frozen cauliflower and ten tons of frozen zucchini! We had to remove the cauliflower and zucchini and distribute them within twenty-four hours. We were able to do this with the assistance of trucking firms taking on the extra load and bringing the frozen food to distribution sites where our member organizations and others were able to give it out to people who were seniors, as well as those who were homeless or had low incomes.

Next, we contacted the hundreds of farms that had food left over after harvests. In the past, farmers had plowed under the leftover crops. We worked with Senior Gleaners, an organization that farmers allowed to glean or pick the leftover crops to give to seniors. We arranged for the organization to pick extra crops to donate to our member organizations, giving us access to fresh foods. The Food Network became a cooperative effort of churches, denominations, food banks, soup kitchens, homeless shelters, local businesses, senior organizations, trucking companies, and local and state governments. It began simply with a group of Christian food banks and soup kitchens and just grew. This was the churches making a difference in their communities. This was the Christian church being the change agent in vulnerable communities.

Interrupting Systemic Racism

In *White Fragility,* author Robin DiAngelo challenges her white readers to think about how they have fit into systemic racism and how they can become anti-racists.[1] She asks them to start by reflecting on their individual experiences of being white. Next, she asks them to redefine racism and their role in a racist system. She calls for white people to become educated on people of color by reading, watching, and listening. Above all, she tells them to be humble and to know there is much to learn.

Interrupting systemic racism will not be easy for anyone, neither white people nor people of color. People of color and whites need to be allies.

In the late 1990s, Rev. Ken Feske and the First Baptist Church of Salinas (a predominantly white church in a mainly Hispanic agricultural community) helped to organize citywide summits to address crucial issues in their community and nearby communities. One issue was rising crime, violence, and gang activity. Community stakeholders (e.g., parents, police, city government officials, health professionals, teachers and school officials, social workers, churches, and other community leaders) were brought together in one place to find solutions. One of the problems they encountered was that, because of the preponderance of issues, people were addressing their problems in isolation. To address that problem, the summits brought people from across the different disciplines together to come up with strategies that were more comprehensive and holistic. For example, if a teenager got into trouble with the police, strategies were put in place to keep the teen out of the criminal justice system. The strategies involved working with the teen's parents, church pastors, health professionals, and, if needed, social workers, the school, and community leaders. Once Rev. Feske and First Baptist built this strong network, it included three school districts, twenty-three schools, 180 businesses, twenty religious congregations, thirty-one service clubs, and more than 22,000 students. From this amazing network, a program eventually developed that effectively reduced crime. —Katie

Alliance Building

Being the change in the community means building alliances with each other and advocating for those who have no voice. An ally (advocate) is someone who is in a non-target group and who stands in the way of and intervenes to stop mistreatment.

Key characteristics: an ally (advocate) is someone who

- Stands in the way: intervenes when oppression or mistreatment occurs
- Interrupts whether or not a target person is in the room
- Encourages a target person to get rid of internalized oppression
- Is outraged by the conditions of any group being targeted
- Is fiercely desirous of building alliances with target group
- Takes the target group's liberation struggles seriously
- Is willing to stand with the target group or, in its absence, in support of its struggles
- Does not forget the target group's humanness
- Understands that target group members internalized some self-hating messages and might be confused about their own humanness sometimes
- Examines ways that target group members have been hurt
- Has looked at how she or he (the bridge person) has been hurt by oppression and is taking steps to heal
- Decides to invite the target group's feelings about having been hurt
- Does not challenge the experiences or impressions about what seems racist, sexist, etc.
- Is bold enough and willing to make mistakes
- Is able to apologize when she or he makes a mistake
- Assumes that the training or teaching she or he got about the target group gets in the way of being truly close
- Does not get stuck in feelings of guilt about being white, male, or other characteristics, but instead celebrates those characteristics

- Recognizes that being a member of a non-target group carries privilege that can be used to help establish a more equitable society
- Honors the target group member both as an individual and as a member of the target group; does not put the target group member in the position to speak for everyone in the target group or to always be the teacher for non-target people on the group's oppression
- Does not expect the target group member to be grateful for her or his acts of alliance; sees these acts as a step in his or her own liberation
- Remembers that among non-targets there is always to be found a history of resistance to oppression and celebrates that

Non-targets must assume that

- They will make mistakes.
- Target people want them as allies.
- It is in the target group's best interest to have them as an ally.
- They are doing the best they can, and more can be done.
- They resist systemic racism.

Target group members must assume that

- They and other members of their group deserve allies.
- Those outside of their group have a sincere desire and vested interest in being their ally.
- Their allies are doing the best they can, given their own oppression.
- They are the expert on their own experiences, and they have valuable information that others need to hear.
- Comparisons of who is more oppressed are not useful.

- Their experience as a target group member contains victories as well as apparent defeats.
- Their allies will make mistakes; they need to continue to expect the best from them.
- They can train whom they wish to be their allies.
- They are the ones to decide when they will do this training of allies.
- The only thing that gets in the way of people acting as allies is allies' own internalized conditioning.

See chapter 32, "Moving Toward Liberation," online. For more personal growth opportunities, see the appendices in the online workbook.

NOTES

1. Robin DiAngelo, *White Fragility: Why It's So Hard for White People to Talk About Racism*. (Boston: Beacon Press, 2018).

Conclusion

I am reminded of a scene in an Indiana Jones movie where Indy is on a ledge looking over a deep chasm and needing to get to the other side. The problem is that there's a huge gap between where he is and where he needs to go. He can't see any bridge that goes across the chasm to the other side. As far as he can see, there is nothing but empty space between his ledge and the other side. He has to put aside his fears and have faith that the bridge is there. He closes his eyes and steps into the empty space. Sure enough, his foot lands on the bridge that leads to the other side. Once he takes that first step, he can see the bridge and walk to the other side.

Building the bridge toward the Beloved Community is like that. We cannot see the bridge at first. The journey seems difficult, fearful, almost impossible. However, once we conquer our anxiety and fears and take the first step in faith, we begin to see the bridge; actually, we build the bridge as we walk.

My hope and prayer for each of you is that you will take the opportunities that God opens up to you to risk being uncomfortable, to take a step of faith into the unknown, to travel on this intercultural journey toward a Beloved Community, and to build the bridges to cross! —Katie

As I reflect on the gospel imperative outlined so clearly in the Scriptures, an image comes of individuals moving forward, step by step, toward a more just society. The energizing element for me in that image is knowing that people are going hand in hand with others—women, men, children, the elderly, those bent over and those standing straight, and people speaking different languages, having different backgrounds, and singing songs together.

I have been drawn my entire adult life to be on this journey of bridging social and cultural differences. In doing so, I slowly and painfully have become attuned to the misunderstanding, the prejudices, the active marginalization, and the tacit oppression of whomever is "the other." Feeling the call of a loving and justice-seeking God, the divine which permeates all of life, my question has been and continues to be, How can I best join with others in the journey toward a Beloved Community? How might I use my identity, background, and interests to be an effective, caring partner in this journey? These are likely the questions for us all when we open ourselves to the Holy Spirit.

Will there be joy in new learning and friendships? Yes! Will there be confusion and misunderstandings? Yes! Will there be questions and new insights? Yes! Will your life expand and deepen? Yes! It is my prayer that this book will support you on your journey to build and delight in intercultural relationships. My hope is that those relationships bring to you the vision and the commitment to be a witness and a healer in our fractured society and in the communities where you live. May you move forward in faith and action with excitement to build bridges of relationships. —Shan

God is a God of diversity. If I think of God as a Baskin-Robbins ice cream store, how bland would the world be if it was all vanilla or chocolate or strawberry? Diversity exists in a variety of forms. The world has many flavors. Psalm 34:8 says, "Taste and see that it is good."

As with anything new, rarely do we dive all in. We take little licks of any new flavor. We are cautious, especially if the flavor is "exotic" and seems strange to us. As one engages in new intercultural relationships, there will be iceberg crashes as mentioned earlier in the book. There will be misjudgments and misunderstandings as we seek to navigate new relationships. Don't run when these occur. Stay, ask questions, learn, and grow. Try these new flavors.

It's okay to go slow. One workshop, one training, one book, will not make you an expert. No matter how many books you read, no matter how many workshops you attend, there is always more to learn. I have pastored five different congregations. What I learned in a previous congregation was helpful but didn't always translate well into the next congregation because cultures are different. The good news is I did not have to start over. I knew questions to ask about what was important to that new cultural group, what were the rituals, what were the important dates to be celebrated, and so on. And most of all, I was more self-aware of my values, my ethnocentrism, and my prejudices and biases.

A mentor once said, "There is no such thing as a stranger, only sisters and brothers we have never met." Learn to become uncomfortable in your discomfort as you meet more of your new family. New worlds will open up to you that you never knew existed. Your life and friendships will become richer and deeper as you do. Enjoy the journey! —Dale

Glossary

A note about our usage of terms and their meanings: Group identity terms used have been and continue to be in flux. The terms used here reflect current usage.

African American/Black American: Current preferred concept referring to citizens of the United States who are of African descent. Usage includes the connection with the nations and cultures of the African continent, many of whose peoples were brought to the United States as slaves. Black American refers to African Americans and Blacks from the Caribbean, West Indies, and Central and South America who are of African descent. It is also the term we use to refer to black immigrants from Africa who may or may not be citizens. Today Black is seen as a term of affirmation.

I am an African American male. I use the terms "African American" and "Black" interchangeably. However, they mean two different things. The term "African American" describes Black people born in the United States who claim their African heritage. It doesn't mean we all want to go live in Africa. It means we recognize our ancestors who came to America on the slave ships, many of them losing their lives in the Middle Passage. Like Italians, Germans, Polish, and others born in the United States, Blacks also can connect our history and ancestry to another land.

I use the term "Black" as a term of pride, as in the lyrics from James Brown's famous song, "I'm Black and I'm proud." Instead of being Negroes, a name given to us by European Americans, we were able to name ourselves in the 1960s. "Black" was and is a term of self-determination.

Yet, the term is much broader. "Black people" is a term usually referring to a racial group of humans with dark skin color, but the term has also been used to categorize a number of diverse populations into one common group. In other words, it doesn't just represent those born in the United States. The term can also include those born in Africa, the Caribbean, and other places around the world. My friends from Africa and Haiti remind me from time to time when I use the term "African American" that they are not included in that term. Thus, Black is more inclusive of the dark-skinned people who have been oppressed, and who are of the African Diaspora. —Dale

American: Used to refer to permanent residents or citizens of the United States. However, this use is presumptuous since it excludes other countries of North, Central, and South America. Technically, persons from all the Americas can be considered Americans.

Asian American: Current preferred concept referring to citizens of the United States who are of Asian descent. Usage includes the connection with the nations and cultures of the Asian continent. Often in the United States the concept has broadened to include not only persons of Asian descent from the Asian nations (i.e., Korea, China, Japan, and the Philippines) but also Southeast Asian countries (i.e., Vietnam, Laos, Cambodia, Thailand, Myanmar), the Asian subcontinent (i.e., India, Pakistan), the Middle East (i.e., Iran, Iraq), and the Pacific Islands (i.e., Samoa, Fuji). Oriental refers to the people and culture of the Orient or East (Asia). However, this term originated from the

Europeans and was used in comparison with the West, Westerner, or occidental. The English used this term in reference to those subject to British colonial rule in Asia and North Africa. Its usage is outdated and is seen as offensive.

Bigotry: An extreme form of prejudice that is intolerant of differences.

BIPOC: Stands for Black, Indigenous, People of Color, and is an acronym used to describe the marginalized and minority groups in the United States. These groups have historically and traditionally been the groups targeted by systemic racism.

Caste: The hierarchal social system in place in the United States and elsewhere in the world. (The most famous example is India's caste system.) The system places different groups of people into specified, defined, and rigid positions in society. The dominant caste in the United States is people of white or European descent. The lowest castes in the United States are black Americans and Native Americans. The other people of color fit into the middle castes. In the United States castes came into play when the first Europeans landed in the new world and when slaves were brought to enrich the dominant caste. Castes have been kept in place by means of historic and systemic racism.

Discrimination: An act based on prejudice, showing differential treatment favoring one group over another. These actions involve denying, limiting, or restricting access to benefits, rights, resources, privileges, and qualities of life. These actions can be intentional or unintentional.

Hispanic/Latinx American: Hispanic is the current preferred concept referring to citizens of the United States who are of Spanish language and descent. Hispanic refers to lineage and language traced to Spain. Latinx refers to individuals whose ancestry is from Central and South America and the Caribbean and speak Spanish and Portuguese (originating from Portugal).

Latinx is in reference to the Latin languages. "X" is non-gender specific instead of the terms "Latino" and "Latina." "Hispanic" is the term the federal government created in 1980 as a census category for persons with Spanish surnames, Spanish as their primary language, or of Spanish descent. Prior to this, the deferral government classified Latino/Latina as "white." Chicano is a term used by many Mexican Americans, reflecting their cultural heritage and identity. Puerto Rican is one of the other major Latin groups in the United States. Although the people of Puerto Rico are citizens of this country, those whose official residence is in Puerto Rico are not permitted to vote in US elections or to have congressional representation. Puerto Rican citizens residing in the fifty states are able to vote and have congressional representation.

Native American: Current preferred term referring to indigenous persons of the United States. Usage includes the connection to indigenous persons living in the United States and persons living in tribal nations within the United States. Often, the concept has been broadened to include indigenous persons living in the Americas, Central America, South America, and Canada. Indigenous refers to the original native populations in different countries. Historically, indigenous persons were categorized as a "Mongoloid race," as opposed to two other categories of "race," "Caucasoid and Negroid." In this country, the federal government recognizes more than three hundred distinct nations and societies. In addition, there are more than two hundred that are not recognized. Indian is a term that originated from Christopher Columbus's mistake in believing that he had reached the Asian continent and India. When he saw the indigenous people, he called them "Indian." "Indian" is also a term used in the United States, such as referring to the "Indian tribes" and "Indian reservations."

Non-target: Groups of people who are recipients of privileged positions of economic, political, social, and religious power.

Non-targets can perpetuate mistreatment either passively or actively, or can take advocacy roles for target groups.

Oppression: The systematic, institutional, pervasive, routine mistreatment, or subjugation of individuals on the basis of their membership in various groups that are disadvantaged by imbalances of power in society or the church.

Pacific Islander (American): Citizens of the United States who are of Pacific Island descent. Usage includes the many persons originating from the nations and cultures of the Pacific Islands. Often, in the United States the connection is broadened to include descendants of the native population of the Maori of New Zealand, Samoa, Tonga, Fiji, Guam, Tahiti, as well as the state of Hawaii. Culturally and ethnically this term refers to peoples of the Polynesian culture.

People of Color/Third World: The current preferred concept for all peoples who are of brown, red, yellow, and black skin hues. Usage connotes a common experience and treatment by whites, Europeans, and European Americans. The common experience and treatment includes prejudice, stereotyping, racism, subjugation, or conquest. "Third world" or the current term "two-thirds world," which recognizes that these nations and cultures comprise the global majority, also refers to the poorer nations of this planet. Non-western refers to people who are not of white European descent.

Prejudice: A judgment, opinion, attitude, or feeling formed beforehand or without adequate knowledge, evidence, thought, or reason, and often done out of emotions. We all have prejudices consciously or subconsciously.

Racism: The belief that one ethnic stock is superior to others and has the power to enforce this view. Prejudice, bigotry, stereotypes, and discrimination are systematically, institutionally, pervasively, and routinely enforced by persons in power who have authority and resources. One description is "prejudice plus power and privilege."

Reverse Oppression: The notion that a person from a non-target group has been mistreated based on belonging to the non-target group. However, oppression is the systematic, institutional, pervasive, routine mistreatment of persons whose group has been disadvantaged by society. Quite the opposite, non-target groups have not been systematically disadvantaged by society.

Stereotype: An oversimplification or untruth about an entire group of people. All individuals of a particular group are categorized together regardless of unique characteristics. Stereotypes are often rooted in inaccurate beliefs. Although some stereotypes are positive on the surface, they affect a particular group negatively by limiting and restricting the group's members.

Target: Groups of people who lack economic, political, social, and religious power. They are recipients of mistreatment.

White/European American: Emerging concept referring to citizens of the United States who are of European descent. Usage includes the connection with the nations and cultures of Europe and the United Kingdom. Historically these are the nations that colonized many parts of the world. Often the connection is broadened to include those descending from other nations and cultures (i.e., Australia, New Zealand, Eastern Europe, Israel, Slavic, and Nordic countries). In the United States they have been the dominant group in population, resources, power, and politics. White or Anglo refers to color and does not appropriately reflect this group since there are Latinx and Native Americans who are "white." Originally, Caucasian referred to the inhabitants of the Caucasus region of Eastern Europe. (There is an old belief that the "Aryan" race originated there.) The term "Caucasian" includes persons inhabiting not only Europe but also northern Africa, southwestern Asia, and the Indian subcontinent. WASP (white, Anglo-Saxon, Protestant) also does not truly reflect this group. There are many European Americans who are not Anglo-Saxon or Protestant. "Western" is another term used to refer to this group. (If this seems confusing, it is.)